The Pursuit *of* GOD

"Catch me if you Can...."

NATALIA "MONIQUE" LEWIS

THE PURSUIT OF GOD
"CATCH ME IF YOU CAN"

Published by Lee's Press and Publishing Company
www.LeesPress.net

All rights reserved, Except for brief excerpts for review purposes, no part of this book may be reproduced or used in any form without written permission from Natalia "Monique" Lewis and/or the publisher.

This document is published by Lee's Press and Publishing Company located in the United States of America. It is protected by the United States Copyright Act, all applicable state laws and international copyright laws. The information in this document is accurate to the best of the ability of Natalia "Monique" Lewis at the time of writing. The content of this document is subject to change without notice.

ISBN-13: 978-1544666167 *Paperback*
ISBN-10: 1544666160

Table of Contents

Dedications i
Introduction.. ii
I'm Chasing After You 1
Catch Me if You Can 11
His Desires Are My Desires 18
I Am…The Good Shepherd.........................24
I'm Under His Shadow 30
Oh, How He Loves You & Me 32
Seeking the Hand of God............................39
Daddy I Love You 42
Something About the Name of Jesus.......46
My First Love 49
I Won't Go Back...54
Yeshua 58
I Almost Let Go 60
No More Fear..63
ZOE "The Life" 66
Stop in the Name of Love 69
Knock, Knock, Knock, It's Me Again 71
Seeking the Heart of God...........................76
God's Heart for the Nations......................80

You Go Girl 83
It's About You 87
My Heart is Crying 89
Seeking the Face of God 91
Back to the Future 96
This Is It 99
To Be Continued 103
Break the Cycle 106
The Price is Right 110
He's Coming Back 113
Your Road to Recovery 117
The Final Rebound 121
The Golden Eagle 125
The Eagle's Mentality 129
Living A Life Full of Passion for God 132
Bibliography 133

Dedication

To my parents the late Elder Glenn Lewis and Nancy Lewis, Grandmother Geraldine Lewis and Nancy Pinkney and Rev. Ruth Taylor.

Introduction

It was spring semester at Oral Roberts University and I was working hard to finish my Master's degree at ORU and anticipating graduation May10, 2007. I was also very excited about *Souls a Fire's* album release that was to be held in March. Yours truly had two songs that were to be released on this album. Blessed Assurance and a song I co-wrote entitled "Be Still". This was the first time my songs were to be released on an album of this caliber. Can you believe that with all these "Glamourous Events" I was struggling internally with depression and experiencing *burnt out syndrome*? I still had the energy but on the inside something was causing me to feel low. What I did not know at that moment was that I had Bipolar Manic Disorder. So, what happened? I just kept doing my usual routine hoping that I would feel better. I ate food but I did not really have an appetite. I remember being on my computer studying for an exam and I was talking to my mother and I said "Mom, I'm not feeling good right now" she said "I'm going to catch a flight to check on you." Two days after my mother arrived in Tulsa I was admitted to Laurette Psychiatric Hospital. Please take a moment and look at this picture. I was 25 years old and I weighed 90 pounds. I thought how did I get here, I'm a believer what happened? I stayed in the hospital for a week and then I went back to NC to recuperate. That was just what I needed.

Everyone was saying the same thing to me "You need to rest, you need to slow down." I agreed with them, yes, I was doing a lot but that was not the problem, the problem was I had too much energy to do all of the above.

When I researched more about my diagnoses my problem was solved. People who have Bipolar Manic Disorder 1 have a surge of energy that they have to be aware of so that they can limit how much they can do. Ok so I am still a youth minister with Bipolar Manic Disorder, does this mean I am not one of those faith believer's anymore? No, it does not. Since I have been diagnosed my faith in God is more than when I accepted him as Lord and Savior of my life. I've had the courage to ask my *Heavenly Father* all my theological questions and the ones that I needed more information on I have explored. One of my hardest questions was the death of my father who succumbed to a heart attack in 2004 and in 2015 my spiritual mentor died. She was a phenomenal teacher and a role model for the next generation. Man, I did not get the memo!

Sometimes in life we do not get the memo. Instead of blaming God I still kept answering the door every time God knocked. I could have relapsed and left what I knew was true about GOD but my glove was still out waiting to hear everything He said. It is now January 14, 2014 and I am still pursuing God. My heart still yearns to hear from him just like when I accepted Him as my Lord and Savior.

Do you still talk to your "Daddy" even when it hurts? The question still remains to be seen. In this book, I will share with you my life experiences and "how to" continue to pursue God beyond your pain. Although sometimes it may seem that God is not near us He has never left a single human being, He is always there… Selah.

I'm Chasing After YOU

Can you believe that God loves you *so much* that He wants all of your undivided attention? He wants you to *run* wholeheartedly after Him to *"Get to Know"* Him for yourself and not through any other person or thing. So many Christians today are comfortable with just worshipping God on Sunday mornings and the passion for God (fire) that they once had on the inside has now begun to dwindle. Instead of *running hard after* God they get so distracted with their careers, social networks, and relationships.

But the Word declares "***There shall have no other gods before me***"(Exodus 20:3). When Christian believers recognize that *Yahweh* is the one and true living God they will no longer want to put any other god before Him. There is no one that can replace the love that we experience from our *"Father."* It is not even worth it to try and trade Him in for another lover.

The *"love"* He gives cannot be pawned at the pawn shop or even put on a book shelf! His love is irreplaceable and we must learn how to rely on Him only to feel our hearts instead of the world. Jesus said, ***"If you know (love) Me then you will keep my commandments and you will not be friends with the world" (John 14:15).*** When you continue to be friends with the world and God, this brings enmity between the covenant relationship you have with Him.

It is impossible to serve two Masters at the same time so make the decision to keep God! (Matthew 6:24) In the Book of Numbers 14:1, God even told the Israelites after bringing them out of the wilderness that He was going to deliverer them into a land of plenty full of milk and honey known as *Canaan*. The only requirement was that they had to continually worship God only and to not serve any other gods. But they were also distracted with serving other idols and that kept them from entering into their promise. When we choose to *run hard after God* we will begin to possess the promises of God that He wants to give to our *generation and the generations to come!* The Israelites missed their land of promise because they wanted to become like other nations instead of choosing to become more like God. In our pursuit of God, we need to *run hard after God*, like Joshua and Caleb who were the only two people able to enter the land of Canaan because they had a different Spirit and they followed God fully with all of their heart (Numbers 14:24). As you start *running hard after God* He will impart (breath) a different Spirit on you and you will not continue to serve other idols that may have previously been a part of your life. *You will have a new ring on your finger that will seal the covenant that you have made with Him as the ruler of your life!*

Seal the deal with the Master! We seal the deal with the Master first by getting to know Him.

A marriage cannot exist if your spouse does not communicate with you. Can you imagine asking questions to your husband or wife and they refuse to respond to you? My friend dating is only an "introduction" but a marriage is a covenant agreement to "Get to know" your significant other for a lifetime.

Just like a marriage when we commit to God we have a covenant agreement to "Get to know Him" on a daily basis. God's ultimate desire (challenge) is for His people to know Him even in the fellowship of His suffering? (Philippians 3:10) When we pursue God we also *"Get to Know Him"* through what He felt on the cross when Christ said **"Father forgive them for they do not understand what they have done"** (Luke 23:34). Christ understood that His death was a sacrifice for humanity to be saved and that His Heavenly Father was going to resurrect Him back with a glorious body. You may be wondering why does God still want me to *"Get to Know Him"* by feeling His pain? But remember Jesus said, **"If you suffer with me, you will reign with me"** (2 Timothy 2:12). God does allow situations to come into our lives for us to depend on Him only and to purge our hearts so that we can see like Him, hear like Him, smell like Him, and speak like Him!

The Book of James encourages every Christian believer to:

"Count it all joy when you face adversities knowing that it is the testing of your faith that will bring patience in your life, and let patience have its perfect work in you so that you will be perfect lacking nothing" (James 1:2-4, and experience brings hope, and our hope in God will not be put to shame). When you *run hard after God* you will learn how to rejoice in the Lord always even when you are in hurt or pain (Philippians 4:4). Peter said, *"Do not be surprised at the painful trial you are suffering, as though something strange were happening to you but rejoice that you participate in the sufferings of Christ so that you may be overjoyed when His glory is revealed"* (1 Peter 4:13) By doing this God will receive all the glory through your situation and you will become an effective witness to others. When you *run hard after God* He will show you ways to evangelize unbelievers by sharing your faith! In the summer of 2009, I remember having a dream about a ship sailing across the ocean and it stopped to it next location. Then I saw myself and my bags were being bought to the ship and said to the Captain "Where are we going?" He said "We are going to several different locations and he began to tell me the list of the locations."

Then I woke up and God said to me "I am preparing you to be sent out as an evangelist (Word and Music) on the mission's field. I have to admit that at that moment I had never been on the mission's field I was only an encourager and a sender to people to help them share the Gospel. I was totally flabbergasted amazed that God would even choose me to carry the Gospel beyond the United States of America and I prayed asking God one are the next steps that I need to take. My heart for God is HUGE, never did I contemplate saying "No" to ever going. I said yes, the moment I woke up from that dream. Is your heart "Big" for sharing his heart with others? The question needs to be asked Do you get excited anymore about telling someone else Christ? What if your answer was I use too but now I do not because I have been interrupted by life? Life can become a distraction to us all being in love with shopping, being in love with my love, being in love with popularity, being in love with my church duties, being in love with being a busybody, being in love with my routine or regime, hey what happened to God who should be first on our To Do List. Before we realize it we have become part of life's To Do List instead of God's Daily News.

Earlier today I was reading a document by Howard Culberson that asked the question *"What will you do in the next five days that will move the Church towards reaching people in the 10/40 with the gospel?"*

(Howard Culbertson, 1). *There are 90% of people who are living in the 10/40 window who have not had the chance to even hear the "Good News" message* (Howard Culbertson, 1). God wants all mankind to be saved in His Kingdom in order to execute His heavenly assignment down here on earth. Although some of us may understand the biblical mandate of God there are still many Christians today who are not fulfilling their assignments because they have lost their passion for the things of God. Last night as I gently laid down on my bed preparing to go to sleep all of a sudden I kept seeing these words come before me in a vision **PERSISTENCE** and **CONSISTENCY.** It was revealed to me by the Spirit instantaneously that both of these words have to be applicable in our daily walk with God. What does it mean to be *persistent?* When we are *persistent* we refuse to give up or let go in our faith journey. Yes, when we are persistent we are persevering continuously for more of GOD in our lives! Have you ever made a cake and forgot to put the sugar in the mix before putting it in the oven? Ok it probably did not taste right because the sugar is one of the main ingredients you need when you are making a cake that you must have. Likewise, in our pursuit of God we have to show God that we are serious in our walk with Him and the assignment that He has called us to accomplish.

In my relationship with my close friends I always make sure that I stay in close proximity with them and that I return their phone calls in a timely manner unless something has happened drastically. By doing this I let them know that I care about each one of them and I am a true friend in their life. God wants to be treated the same way because He wants our full attention.

God wants to be treated the same way because He wants our full attention. On a continual basis, we should always communicate with our "Father" and through our persistence in our Christian walk we show Him that we are true to His covenant that He first made to us. God wants to be the "best" entertainer in our lives and He wants us to use the remote control to turn on His television and watch His channel. When we pursue God wholeheartedly we will be living *the best days of our lives!* **What does it mean be consistent as a believer?** It's when our behavior exemplifies the character of God over a long period of time.

In other words, as a Christian believer you will be able to stand on the word of God and having done all that you know how to do you will continue to STAND! There are too many Christians jumping ship before obtaining all that God has promised for them. We have to know within our heart that ***God is able to do exceedingly, abundantly, far above all that we can ever ask, imagine, or think according to the power that works in us!*** (Eph. 3:20). There are certain situations in our life that demand us to rise up and command our promise.

Regardless of what we see with our natural eyes we have to be like a tree planted by the river of water that will bring forth our fruit in due season **(Psalm 1:3).** As you are reading this book, I want you to know that as you stand on the word of God He has a due season for you and God is a rewarder of those who *consistently* seek Him! **(Hebrews 11:6)**

We have all had friends and family members that have come in and out of our life for various reasons and some of them would make promises that fail to come to pass. Some of them would say *"Things are going to be different this time"* and they still did not change just imagine how God feels if we keep making promises to Him and never totally give Him our all (never fulfilling our promises to Him).

Think about it God never fails to wake us up in the morning or to make sure that we have breath in our body. God keeps His promises and in return we should keep our promises to Him.

As a child of the King we should want to give Him all the worship and praise that He deserves and turn our lives completely to Him. When we are consistent in our relationship with God it should cause us to break ties from unhealthy and ungodly relationships. We should on a daily basis cry out to God for Him to break away every soul tie and generational curses that has been a familiar stronghold in our life. We should not feel comfortable doing Christianity but we need to "be" (become) Christ-like.

I heard someone say *"Yes I am doing the church thing now or I am trying the church thing now!"* Christianity is about having a pure relationship with the Lord and not allowing anyone to break that connection between you and the King! There is a song called *"Praise is what I do"* and there is a stanza in the song that says, "I vow to praise you through the good and the bad, I'll praise you whether *happy or sad because praise is what I do."* In our commitment to the Lord through the Holy Spirit we can still be content in an awful situation and still lift our hands and praise God even when it hurts! When we continually praise God while we are going through it shows Him that we love Him because He is God. The three Hebrew boys uttered to King Nebuchadnezzar ***"Even if He does not deliver us from this fiery furnace we know that He is still able"*** **(Daniel 3:17).**

When we are consistent in God we have *"unshakeable faith"* and we take a rightful position in Heavenly places with Christ and when this happens it releases what God has given to us here on earth (2 Timothy 1:12; Galatians 2:16).

Just like in the military there are certain armed positions that the soldier must take in order to protect themselves and the team in our pursuit of God we have to stay armed on the battlefield so that the enemy will not attack you or the body of Christ.

When we show God that we are serious about His Kingdom then He knows that He can trust us even more. **"If we remain faithful over a few things then He will make us ruler over much!"** (Matthew 25:23)

Confession: *I am consistent in every area of my life as it pertains to the will of God. I close every doorway or soul tie that has been a distraction to my relationship with God. I totally trust you God and as a sacrifice I will give you my time, my family, my worship, my career, and all my affairs. Cover me with your wings and create in me a clean heart, renew the right spirit on the inside of me. I choose to pursue you over everything and your plan for my life. In Jesus Name. Amen.*

Catch Me If You Can

Have you ever hungered and thirsted just for one Word from God? You fasted and you prayed just longing to be close to Him to feel His presence. Our Heavenly Father desires for all of His children to seek His face, to seek His hand, and to seek His heart. There is nothing like being in the presence of God! But there are times when we chase after God and we do not sense Him there because He is silent. Just when you need an immediate answer to get direction or need to know how to handle the fact that you were dismissed on your job God chooses to be silent. What do you do? My friend you continue to pray, praise, and seek the face of your God who will never leave you or forsake you even when He is silent (Deuteronomy 31:6). How do we continue to seek God's face when He is silent? It seems as if He is rejecting me because I do not hear Him, or feel Him near me, is God ignoring me? Is God playing the game *"Hide, Go, and Seek with me?"* As soon as I think I have figured Him out then He goes and hides again… Ok God I am getting tired of chasing after you around this house. I remember when I was a child I use to play the game Hide, Go, and Seek." Sometimes in our Christian walk it may seem that God is playing the Game but He really isn't. It can be us running instead of Him sometimes running and hiding from Him. We are supposed to run and seek after God and although sometimes you were tired of trying to find little Johnny you wanted to win the game so bad you went the extra mile until you found him! In the same manner, there are challenges in life that we face so that God can test our faith to see if we are going to go the extra mile to find Him. He does hear us when we call His name although sometimes looking at our circumstances we may ask the question **"GOD WHERE ARE YOU?"** This rhetorical question was also asked by our friend Job. But when we thoroughly examine Job's story we can see that God was there all the time. He actually told Satan to test Him on account that He knew that he was an *upright man*. Instead of cursing God when the test became unbearable and Job too faced one tragedy after the next he began to cry out to the Lord for saying:

"My soul is weary of my life, I will leave my complaint upon myself; I will speak in the bitterness of my soul, I will say to God do not condemn me, show me what I have done wrong, is it good for you to keep me in this oppression, do you despise the work of your hands, God I really have done nothing wrong." **(Job 10: 1-7)**

We may have felt the same way Job did failing to realize that God's presence or His hand was ever present in our life. God sometimes plays catch with us by throwing us balls from eternity and we have the gloves in our hands receiving from Him.

Regardless of where you are placed on His field please do not stop seeking and chasing after God! We must continually seek God through every challenge and adversity in life we undergo. Our maximum potential is developed in the areas that we feel the most crushed and stretched beyond our normal measures. When we have exhausted all possibilities for our present situation is the time where God will push all the new ideas, skills, and talents He has given! Even writing this book now I am a witness that God has totally changed my life from being on the sidelines to becoming a partner in the game we call *Kingdom Life*.

We Cry Abba Father
What do you do when your heart has been broken into two pieces because you lost a father, a mother, your spouse, your daughter, your son, or your mentor? You have experienced a tragedy and no one and no place can replace that individual. I've been there and I cry "ABBA FATHER." Daddy I cannot do anything else but cry. You cry until the tears can no longer come down your eyes and you feel like God failed you. Is God still there? You ask because you put so much trust in Him and this is not going to be a lost story without a cause or effect. You count one, two, three, four because that makes sense but now it is no longer one, two, or three its 25, 29, and then Zero 0. Have you ever felt like a 0? I have no number because I do not feel like I have a life ANYMORE.

But greater is he that is in you than he that is in the WORLD (1 John 4:4). You may feel like living life or receiving God's daily news is no longer worth it and then the Holy Spirit strengthens you by giving you a flashback from the past. If he did it before then he can definitely do it again. Thank you Tye Tribett for that song that reminds us that the Greater One lives in us that will cause us once again to STAND. Physically when we get up our feet have to support us so that we can stand. What if I told you that your spiritual feet can never be cut off? Your feet are like an eagle's so that spiritually you will soar far above what we call life's elevators because God still gives His daily news. Even though there are some balls that we do not want to catch from life we still have the strength to hold on to the baseball glove. As I close this chapter, take a brief moment to meditate on these scriptures and imagine yourself with a baseball glove in your right hand raised to the sky wanting to catch God's ball.

Matthew 6:33 (AMP) But seek (aim at and strive after) first of all His kingdom and His righteousness (His way of doing and being right), and then all these things taken together will be given to you.

1 Chronicles 15:13 (AMP) For because you bore it not [as God directed] at the first, the Lord our God broke forth upon us--because we did not seek Him in the way He ordained.

1 Chronicles 28:9 (AMP) And you, Solomon my son, know the God of your father [have personal knowledge of Him, be acquainted with, and understand Him; appreciate, heed, and cherish Him] and serve Him with a blameless heart and a willing mind. For the Lord searches all hearts and minds and understands all the wanderings of the thoughts. If you seek Him [inquiring for and of Him and requiring Him as your first and vital necessity] you will find Him; but if you forsake Him, He will cast you off forever.

2 Chronicles 15:2 (AMP) And he went out to meet Asa and said to him, hear me, Asa, and all Judah and Benjamin: The Lord is with you while you are with Him. If you seek Him [inquiring for and of Him, craving Him as your soul's first necessity], He will be found by you; but if you [become indifferent and] forsake Him, He will forsake you.

2 Chronicles 17:3 (AMP) The Lord was with Jehoshaphat because he walked in the first ways of his father [David]. He did not seek the Baals.

Psalm 69:32 (AMP) The humble shall see it and be glad; you who seek God, inquiring for and requiring Him [as your first need], let your hearts revive and live!

Hosea 2:7 (AMP) And she shall follow after her lovers but she shall not overtake them; and she shall seek them [inquiring for and requiring them], but shall not find them. Then shall she say, let me go and return to my first husband, for then was it better with me than now.

Leviticus 19:30-32 (AMP) Turn not to those [mediums] who have familiar spirits or to wizards; do not seek them out to be defiled by them. I am the Lord your God.

Deuteronomy 4:29 (AMP) But if from there you will seek (inquire for and requires of necessity) the Lord your God, you will find Him if you truly seek Him with all your heart [and mind] and soul and life.

Deuteronomy 12:5 (AMP) But you shall seek the place which the Lord your God shall choose out of all your tribes to put His Name and make His dwelling place, and there shall you come.

1 Samuel 25:29 (AMP) Though man is risen up to pursue you and to seek your life, yet the life of my lord shall be bound in the living bundle with the Lord your God. And the lives of your enemies-them shall He sling out as out of the center of a sling.

1 Samuel 28:6 (AMP) When Saul inquired of the Lord, He refused to answer him, either by dreams or by Urim [a symbol worn by the priest when seeking the will of God for Israel] or by the prophets.

1 Kings 18:10 (AMP) As the Lord your God lives, there is no nation or kingdom where my lord has not sent to seek you. And when they said, He is not here; he took an oath from the kingdom or nation that they had not found you.

1 Kings 19:10 (AMP) He replied, I have been very jealous for the Lord God of hosts; for the Israelites, have forsaken Your covenant, thrown down Your altars, and killed Your prophets with the sword. And I, I only, am left; and they seek my life, to take it away.

His Desires Are My Desires

What a powerful statement that denotes such spiritual maturity when *His desires become our desires.* When His desires become our desires our lives begin to match our words and actions and this will impact the world! We will be much more effective witnesses in the Kingdom of God! I have to be completely honest with you and admit that this was a major challenge in my personal relationship with God for several years. God had to really infuse my heart to hear His heart beat! I had to finally address the hard questions that all of us at some point tend to run from and really think about questions like what is God's will for my life? What is His purpose and call for my life? Is He pleased with my life? These were the questions that like clock-work replayed in my spirit every day and compelled me to have to eventually allow God to change my life's manuscript. I admit I wrote my own manuscript for how my life was going to be and for a course of my life I was consumed by my own *heart's desires*.

As believers, we have to know that there is a distinct difference in what is in a man's heart or woman's heart from what is in God's heart-beat. For centuries, we have been misinterpreting the scripture ***"He will give you the desires of your heart."*** In the Amplified Bible it reads, ***"Delight yourself also in the Lord, and He will give you the desires and secret petitions of your heart" (Psalm 37:4).***

This text actually means that God has to be at the very center of our heart's desire. He has to take the time to transform the stony heart that we once had so we will have His desires for our life. Ezekiel 36:26 says, *"A new heart I give you and a new spirit will I put within you and I will take away the stony heart out of your flesh and give you a heart of flesh."* Then our heart will be able to submit to the plan He made for our lives and we will put our faith only in Him. In our pursuit of God, we have to get to the place (disposition) where we are totally content in Him and where we do not allow any other person or thing to take His place. Philippians 11-12 says, "Being filled with the fruits of righteousness, which are by Jesus Christ, unto the glory and praise of God. But I would have you understand that thing which happened has happened because of me sharing the Gospel of Jesus Christ so that the Gospel would be positioned and my Father would be glorified." God totally changed Paul's heart from being a heart of a stone until it became HUGE for the cause of Christ. He no longer was this religious felon who murdered Christians but he became an Apostle to the believers. While reading this book, you may want to ask God to take the stone out of your heart and make your heart HUGE for Him. Well he's listening just ask Him. Then listen for his instruction.

When we read the Book of Solomon he says, *"But the beginning of wisdom is the sincerest desire for God's instruction and concern for instruction and concern*

for instruction is to love it" (Proverbs 6:17). When your heart's desire is to live for Him you will continue to seek His face for *the wisdom* that leads to life in His Kingdom! (Proverbs 6:11) In this *postmodern world*, many people seek the truth from mediums, false religions, the media, searching for the most populated new concept to bid on. There are over 4, 200 religions (Adherents.com, 1) in this entire world and the world is still searching to know more about religion instead of simply having a relationship with God. The definition of religion is the belief in and worship of a superhuman controlling power in person or gods. Religion is full of pious acts or charitable expression instead of just sharing who Christ is and revealing His character (google.com, page 1). Christianity is based solely on a relationship with Christ and revealing His Character. In Christianity, we accept the fact that we are only perfect through Christ so we will make mistakes but it is the grace of God that causes us not to be consumed. We will never be good enough, or great enough, but we can do all things through Christ who strengthens us (Philippians 4:13). Also, we will never know the entire plan that God has for our lives but we still trust Him that we can reach for the STARS.

At the age of 12, I remember my friends and I would be in church playing the game M.A.S.H. we would all plan our lives on a piece of scratch paper (Yes in church! LOL BORED). We would to choose where we would live, who we would marry, what age we would get married, what car we would drive, what career we would have, how many children we would have, and what age we would have our children! Yes, we were all playing the *Game of Life*. As we grew up we quickly came to the understanding that our lives were not our own.

In **Galatians 2:20 (AMP),** the Apostle Paul said, ***"I have been crucified with Christ [in Him I have shared His crucifixion]; it is no longer I who live, but Christ (the Messiah) lives in me; and the life I now live in the body I live by faith in (by adherence to and reliance on and complete trust in) the Son of God, who loved me and gave Himself up for me."***

Have you ever eaten a pop-tart after you put them in a toaster? They taste very good. Did you have to put icing on the pop-tart? No, you did not. It's already there. In this same manner, your desires are there because God put them in your heart. How do you distinguish your desires from God's desires that's a good question? There are three components that need to be addressed 1. Do you have the ability or the talent? 2. It needs to be God-centered 3. It needs to be confirmed prophetically. For example, if you are a great singer you have the desire to record an album. God will already have in the plan a recording contract, you already have the ability and the desire to record. God put it there. Another example, I have the desire to buy a certain house, well you made a huge amount of money in real estate so you can afford this specific house. God is a logical God. This means that He does not always tell someone to buy a house that they will never be able to afford. What if I thought God told me that this particular man was supposed to be my husband and he married another woman? Can this really happen? Well we have to understand that God gave us all free will. It does not mean that he did not have a desire for you. But if God said it there needs to be a confirmation that he is interested in you. If he is not remotely interested in you then it could be your flesh telling you that. So, we have to make sure that first he is interested in you, and that it does not defy the laws of God (God-centered), meaning that he is not having sex with women or he's not already another woman's husband and it is prophetically confirmed. Every decision that we make needs to be approved by God. God truly loves for His children to seek Him diligently and then He will reward them openly. How do we diligently seek God? To be *diligent* means to be constant in effort to accomplish something; attentive and persistent in doing anything; For example, when we do a particular task it should be done and pursued with persevering attention, we need to give special notice to every detail so that God will be pleased (Dictionary.com, Page 1). ***For whoever finds me finds life, and obtains favor from the Lord, but those who miss me injure themselves; all who hate me love death*** (Prov. 8: 35, 36, AMP). So together let's continue to seek God and watch Him give us the desires of our heart (Psalm 37:4) I would like you now to mediate on Psalm 37:4 and listen to a worship song.

I Am…. The Good Shepherd

Jesus came to seek and save that which was lost. Do you remember the parable Jesus gave to His disciples about the lost sheep? Jesus declared, ***"When 1 of the 99 sheep was lost a Good Shepherd will seek after that one?"*** (Matthew 18:12, AMP). Likewise, our Savior came to seek those who were lost to become saved those who were sick to be healed. He longs to be the shepherd of our lives. Regardless of the fact that Jesus had 99 sheep to watch over, He was still concerned about the 1 who went astray. A *Good Shepherd* takes care of his flock, he protects His flock, and does not allow any of his sheep to go astray. He carries that rod to assure that this will not happen to any of His sheep. When we accept Christ as our Lord and Savior we give Him the permission to become the *"Good Shepherd"* over our lives. At this point He can guide us down the road or towards the plan He has for us instead of being controlled by man. He gives us a *new peace* that we have never experienced before that passes all our finite understanding that we cannot explain to others. People may ask you occasionally how can you truly have "*Peace in the Midst of Your Storm*?" You do not know how to fully describe it so you just say it is a *"peace"* that lives on the inside of me. *"The Good Shepherd"* will lead you beside the still and quiet waters and his staff will comfort you no matter where you go (Psalm 23:4).

He is the God of all comfort and He will keep you from all evil. When we choose to pursue Him as our *"Good Shepherd"* we will see His goodness in our lives and that our cup will overflow (Psalm 23:5).

The Good Shepherd cares about all of His children. Every fraction, every decimal point of our innermost being has not gone unnoticed (or unseen) by Him. He has even counted how many hairs that are actually on our heads (Luke 12:7). He cares about you but do you care about Him? Did you take the time to seek His face, to hear Him tell you today that I love you my daughter or my son? Did you take the time to tell Him how your day was or write him a love-letter? Have you ever heard God singing in your ear or sharing a nursery rhyme to you before you went to bed? If you are reading this book and you are married you know how your husband or wife shares their most intimate secrets with you, God desires that same attention and agape love too! While you are lying together in bed this is the time that he will share with you his heart hoping that you will listen. The bedroom represents your sanctuary, *your intimacy or the communion* that you have with one another and it is not just about your sexual experiences. God desires us to not just penetrate with Him but He wants us to learn how to commune with him on an everyday basis. One of my most intimate times I recall with a guy I used to date was when we talked all night long on the sofa in the dark before he took me to the airport at 4:00am.

I had never ever experienced this before and on the inside I was like "WOW!" I have to confess that I was so afraid at first going over to his apartment thinking that he was not going to be a gentleman but to my surprise He WAS! This man really listened to me and I listened to him. Did you know that God is a *Gentlemen t*oo? He desires to listen to you and He wants you in return to listen to Him! Jesus said, ***"My sheep know my voice or are acquainted (familiar) with my voice and not a stranger"*** (John 10:27) When we listen to God that means that we are adhering to His instructions and we become more intimate with Him. Did you know that the word *submission* really means to listen to someone or something? It comes from the Greek word *hupakoe* meaning to be attentive and in compliance with authority (Strong's Greek Lexicon, 1). Just like a class when the teacher writes on the board and the class immediately stops talking because they have been trained to do so. We take the time to read the board to see what the teacher's lesson is going to be for that specific day in the same manner, God is our teacher. We must listen attentively to hear for direction and also to know what lesson he is teaching us. God also has a lesson plan even if it is to be silent. Most students do not want to be put in detention. We also do not want to be disciplined by God. Instead of being disciplined it would be better if we would get the lesson the first time.

Timothy understood this Biblical principle and he submitted to the mentorship of the Apostle Paul who would often tell him, *"Do not let anyone look down on you because you are young, but set an example for the believers in speech, in life, in love, in faith, and in purity"* (1 Timothy 1:12). He did not look at the Apostle Paul just as any other ordinary man but he submitted to him in obedience to the Lord. As a result, Paul and Timothy developed a *Father and Son* covenant-relationship with one another and Timothy was trained to be able to take care of God's flock. Paul gave specific instructions to Timothy in order to strengthen the churches he said:

"Command those who are rich in this present world not to be arrogant nor to put their hope in wealth, which is so uncertain but to put their hope in God who richly provides us with everything for our enjoyment. Command them to do good, to be rich in good deeds, and to be generous and willing to share. In this way, they will lay up treasure for themselves as firm foundation for the coming age, so that they many take hold of the life that is truly life. Timothy, guard what has been entrusted to your care."

When you listen to God's instructions it can be very rewarding! As you draw closer to God your heart will become *more sensitive* to hear His voice and you will be able to submit to Him without it being a struggle. I am pretty sure that you have previously encountered moments where there was an inner struggle for you to even consider listening to God yet alone obeying Him. You probably quickly found out that disobedience to God can be a rough road to travel with all the bumps, the curves and intersections. They are not fun to endure without having His help to keep us from crashing! Who wants to keep having car accidents and to pay excessive fees on the insurance? NO WAY! A life of obedience leads to a road *full of life* and *prosperity* there will not be any road blocks or destruction that God cannot handle. His angels will be there to guide and protect you every step of the way. Please stay close to your "Daddy" so He can reveal to you His innermost secrets. It will save you from experiencing a lot of heartache and pain. You owe it to yourself. As I close this chapter, please meditate on these Biblical scriptures that deal with our obedience to God.

Proverbs 8

¹Does skillful and godly wisdom cry out, and understanding raise her voice [in contrast to the loose woman?

²On the top of the heights beside the way, where the paths meet, stands Wisdom [skillful and godly;

³At the gates at the entrance of the town, at the coming in at the doors, she cries out:

⁴To you, O men, I call, and my voice is directed to the sons of men.

⁵O you simple and thoughtless ones, understand prudence; you [self-confident] fools, be of an understanding heart.

⁶Hear, for I will speak excellent and princely things; and the opening of my lips shall be for right things.

⁷For my mouth shall utter truth, and wrongdoing is detestable and loathsome to my lips.

⁸All the words of my mouth are righteous (upright and in right standing with God); there is nothing contrary to truth or crooked in them.

⁹They are all plain to him who understands [and opens his heart], and right to those who find knowledge and live by it.

¹⁰Receive my instruction in preference to [striving for] silver, and knowledge rather than choice gold, ¹⁴I have counsel and sound knowledge, I have understanding, and I have might and power.

I'm Under His Shadow

I remember in 2007 and 2010 when I was admitted twice to a psychiatric hospital, the Lord kept letting me know that I was under His shadow and I was going to be released from that place because He was going to restore my mind. The Almighty God has a way of sweeping us right up out of every snare of the enemy. I worshipped God every day until the presence of the Lord breathed upon me and my unstable mind became completely healed, renewed, and transformed by the power of God! Who would have ever thought that six months later God would then launch me on the mission's field in Montego Bay, Jamaica in June 2011 winning souls for Christ with Cruise for a Cause! As being partakers of Christ, God has made an allegiance with His children to protect and keep them in His secret place for His divine purpose for Heaven's divine will to be executed! We pledge allegiance now to everything and anyone else but God. It's time for you to decide now to pledge allegiance to the one who created you, the one who formed you, and knew you before you were in your mother's womb! (Jeremiah 1:5) How dare we pledge allegiance to our country and forget the one who made the country! Even if you are in an incarceration unit, the purpose and the plan of God will still prevail in your life if you just accept!

His ways are not our ways, His thoughts are not our thoughts, and we have been called by the High Priest whose mandate has eliminated every wicked plot of the enemy over our very lives.

Every day when we wake up in the morning we have the opportunity no matter where we are to choose to live out our God given assignment and we are protected by the wings of God! ***"Be Still and Know that He is God"*** (Psalm 46:10). When you abide in the presence of God under His shadow YOU ARE still and not easily moved by every circumstance that you face, or every wind that blows your way. Although the rain pours and the wind blows you are not shaken because YOU ARE under His shadow (Psalm 91:1). When I looked up the definition of a *shadow* it means to be a reflection or an actual mirror that reflects behind you! God's shadow is around us and it moves in rotation everywhere we go! Can you imagine that? I came to tell you today, every inch of movement that you make when you get up in the morning is covered by God and His angelic hosts. You are God's beloved and He watches you like an eagle's eye watches over His hens. You live beneath His wings. As I close this chapter, please meditate on Psalm 91 and listen to the worship song "No Weapon Formed Against You will prosper." (Fred Hammond)

Oh, How He Loves You & Me

Dancing with the Stars is a phenomenal realty television show featuring talented dancers all over the world that compete for a grand prize. All the contestant's family and friends all gather together to support them with great expectation! It is a very exciting show to watch because we can feel the love and the joy of each contestant when they hit the stage. Dancing is one of the best outward expressions of love that we can show towards one another.

Now let's deal with the three types of love that we can express to one another *Eros, Phlileo, and Agape. Eros* is the love that God created between a husband and his wife (Youngblood, 775). In the book of Song of Solomon, we can read the beautiful romantic poems that he wrote to his wife sharing his innermost passionate feelings and love that he had for her. He says to her: **"Let me kiss you for your love is better than wine"** (Song of Solomon 1:1). Even Solomon understood that the love he had for her could also be expressed in an eloquent and romantic ballroom dance. He says, **"Dance, dance, dear Shulammite, Angel Princess! Dance and we'll feast our eyes on your grace! Everyone wants to see the Shulammite dance her victory dances of love and peace** (Song of Solomon 6:13). Solomon gives us the true meaning of what it really means to *fall in love* as a husband and wife. So, next time when your spouse tells you *"Let's go dancing sweetie"* you should get excited because what he's really saying is *"I'm in love with you and I want to show you how I feel in a more intimate way."*

In contrast to this, the term *Phileo* has a two-fold meaning that refers to "the *love* that you have for your everyday relationships such as your friends and also the strong emotional love a parent has for a child (Youngblood, 775). It is a bond between the parent and the child that cannot be broken. In an article, I was reading someone asked Mother Theresa "what society could do to promote world peace? She responded, Go home and love your family" (**www.christianfathers.com**, 1). The word of God teaches us to train our children up in the ways of the Lord and to nurture them by spending quality time with each one of them (Proverbs 22:6). Susie Cortright said, "When my daughter and I were living with my parents awaiting Calliope's birth, Grandpa would announce his arrival each evening with two quick horns. *"Grandpa, Grandpa!"* Cassie would run to the doors so fast that her socks would send her sliding across the linoleum" (**www.christianfathers.com**, 1).

The same love that our parents have for their children, God has for His bride! At the wedding reception before the husband gets the opportunity to caress and dance with his bride we see the beautiful scene of the bride dancing with her father. I remember crying at one of my best friend's wedding during that moment because it was so sacred. Can you imagine having a loving father from the time of your birth? See you develop into the woman of God you were to become? All the nurturing He has given you is being released to your husband? Yes, that is a sacred moment but still there is no greater love than our Heavenly Father has for all His children, it is the *agape love*. Our Heavenly Father's love is kind, patient, forgiving, unfailing, and unconditional. His love will stand the test of time!

The Love Potion
The Love Potion #9 is one of those romantic comedies that was released in 1959 in this movie we would watch young men and women *fall in love* with one another from one drop of a mixed dosage in a drink. What makes this movie so hilarious is when we see the different types of couples dating that would not be what we call the *"Perfect Match."* Watching this movie gives us the opportunity to see a whole different social class, *"The Nerds"* who fall in love with the most popular young men and women in their university. It gives people a new insight that *love* is not always the status quo but *love* is really in the eye of the beholder and notice that when quoting I did not say *"Beauty is in the eye of the beholder* (Molly Bawn, 1878). What I am communicating is that the attraction or fascination that we have for the person *that* we are dating is only to draw us to our *God-mates* but *God's love* will always keep us there. There are many people who cannot distinguish between beauty and love for this reason they use the phrase

"I am not in love with him or her anymore because we have grown apart." I am not talking about for abusive relationships or for an infidelity reason but just relationships that fall apart because the *"Love really was not there in the beginning."* When we take the time to first love God and ourselves we can discern if a person really loves us in the beginning or if it is just an infatuation. The love that God has for His people will never change and it will overcome a multitude of sins (1Peter 4:8). As we learn to embrace His love every day we will become better love makers to Him. God has a *Love Potion #9* that will make our heart's melt and fill us with His everlasting joy! As I close this chapter, please mediate on the song "Falling in love with Jesus." (Jonathon Butler)

Dance with Your Heavenly Father
Have you ever thought how it would be to dance with Jesus? Have you ever danced with God before? When we dance with our father we can reach for the stars of His majesty and intimacy with Him. Just the other day, I was sharing with my friends that I have become so intimate in my time with God that when He finally releases my husband in my life I am not going to know how to handle myself! Now I told God you are going to have to help me because I can truly spend my entire day-off being in the presence of God and dancing with Him. Luther Vandross wrote a song called *"Dance with my Father"* as he was reminded

of his childhood and the innocence of those times with his earthly father. Let's take a moment to look at what he had to say about his relationship with his father.

"Dance with My Father" by Luther Vandross

Back when I was a child, before life removed all the innocence
My father would lift me high and dance with my mother and me and then
Spin me around 'til I fell asleep
Then up the stairs he would carry me
And I knew for sure I was loved
If I could get another chance, another walk, another dance with him
I'd play a song that would never, ever end
How I'd love, love, love
To dance with my father again
When I and my mother would disagree
To get my way, I would run from her to him
He'd make me laugh just to comfort me
Then finally make me do just what my mama said
Later that night when I was asleep
He left a dollar under my sheet
Never dreamed that he would be gone from me
If I could steal one final glance, one final step, one final dance with him
I'd play a song that would never, ever end
'Cause I'd love, love, love
To dance with my father again
Sometimes I'd listen outside her door
And I'd hear how my mother cried for him
I pray for her even more than me

> I pray for her even more than me
> I know I'm praying for much too much
> But could you send back the only man she loved
> I know you don't do it usually
> But dear Lord she's dying
> To dance with my father again
> Every night I fall asleep and this is all I ever dream

Can't you imagine his love for his earthly father in this song? He never wanted to stop dancing with his dad and would often dream about having that moment with him over and over again. God wants us to dance with Him to share in those intimate moments too so that He can take away any trace of emptiness from our lives. When we run after God we show Him our love. The Bible says in Isaiah 55:6, ***"Seek the Lord while he may be found; call on Him while he is near."*** During this time Jerusalem had been ruined and the people needed to be fully restored. The prophet Isaiah kept telling the people to keep worshiping God (keep dancing) because He was going to restore Jerusalem from being ruined. When we dance with God we *worship Him in all of His majesty and glory He will make all things new*! (Nelson Illustrated Bible, Isaiah 55:6, p. 607). ***"When you dance with God "You will go out in joy and be led in peace; the mountains and hills will burst into songs before you, and all the trees of the field will clap their hands. Instead of the thorn bush will grow the pine tree, ad instead of briers the myrtle will grow!"*** (Isaiah 55:14).

We should not ever be ashamed of *dancing with our Daddy because He said* you are ashamed of me and my words the Son of Man will be ashamed of them when he comes in his glory and in the glory of the holy angels (Like 9:26). David's relationship was so intimate with God that He even danced out of His clothes (2 Samuel 6:14) It is very significant that we know that David was first a worshipper before He was a psalmist or musician. He loved to dance with His Heavenly Father" for this reason God told him that he was a man chasing after My heart! David's love for God caused him to become a dancer. Are you a dancer? Will you share your love for God for all the world to see? As I close this chapter, I challenge you to become a dancer like David. Find your favorite praise song and dance before God tonight.

Seeking the Hand of God

In 1 Corinthians 12, the Apostle Paul speaks on the significance of every part of the body of Christ and he uses an analogy comparing the spiritual body to our physical body parts such as the knee, the head, the hand, and etc. The essence of his message is that the body of Christ needs each part to function and has equal importance with Christ being the Head of the Church. In the same manner, when we pursue God we not only seek His face but we also seek His hand. What would you do if you no longer had your hands on your body? For many of us this would be a detrimental situation because our hands play a major role in every aspect of our lives. For example, we praise God with our hands, we cook with our hands, we clean with our hands, we put on our clothes with our hands, ladies we put on our make-up with our hands, we are caretakers with our hands, we administrate with our hands, we work with our hands every minute of the day and night! So take this same concept and imagine spiritually as you are pursuing God's face and neglecting to pursue His hand what would happen? When we seek God's hand that is when we see miracles take place! In the Book of Acts 8:7, "*While Philip was ministering to many people in Samaria they were healed from all kinds of disease and demonic spirits were cast out.*" God's hand is His distribution center and our anchor as His children.

It represents His authority and His majesty. He is King above every king *and Lord above every lord and* ***every knee shall bow down and every tongue shall confess that He is Lord*** (Philippians 2:10). We represent God's enabling power in the Kingdom of God and as *citizens of Heaven* we are joint heirs with Christ who is seated at the right hand of the Father. Abraham, a joint-heir being the Father of many nations, by faith received the promise not through his own righteousness. We are the seed of Abraham, this means that we are his family so we are also joint-heirs to the promise that was given to Abraham. When we are right-standing with God we are not just wealthy but we have a spiritual inheritance for our generation and the next generations. I challenge you today, to seek the right hand of the Father and become part of God's spiritual family to become a joint-heir with Abraham. His hand is His provision, His hand is miraculous, His hand is a spiritual inheritance, and above all His hand represents you and I, His children. We are His family. As I close this chapter, I would like for you to mediate on the scriptures that deal with the hand of God.

1 Peter 5:6 (ESV) "Humble yourselves, therefore, under the mighty hand of God so that at the proper time he may exalt you."

Ezra 8:21-23 (ESV) Then I proclaimed a fast there, at the river d, that we might humble ourselves before our God, to seek from him a safe journey for ourselves, our children, and all our goods. For I was ashamed to ask the king for a band of soldiers and horsemen to protect us against the enemy on our way, since we had told the king, "The hand of our God is for good on all who seek him, and the power of his wrath is against all who forsake him." So, we fasted and implored our God for this, and he listened to our entreaty.

Psalm 110:1 (ESV) The Lord says to my Lord: "Sit at my right hand, until I make your enemies your footstool."

1 Peter 3:22 (ESV) Who has gone into heaven and is at the right hand of God, with angels, authorities, and powers having been subjected to him.

Ezekiel 1:3 (ESV) The word of the Lord came to Ezekiel the priest, the son of Buzi, in the land of the Chaldeans by the Chebar canal, and the hand of the Lord was upon him there.

John 1:3 (ESV) All things were made through him, and without him was not anything made that was made.

Daddy I Love You!

Have you ever experienced as a child your daddy rocking you to sleep? Do you remember how that felt? Or if you did not have that experience did you ever wonder how that would feel? To feel so safe and so loved in the arms of your daddy and sometimes when he would play with you and throw you up in the air you would say, *"Daddy I love You!"*

In the same manner, David developed that same kind of intimacy with God and he was a worshipper. There are several accounts that we see David in the Book of Psalms just telling God how much He loved Him and how He was the lover of his soul. When we love God we love Him with all our heart, mind, strength, and soul! There is a song entitled "I love You Jesus" and some of the lyrics say the following: "I love you Jesus, I worship and adore you, just want to tell you," and this is the powerful part that "I love you more than anything!" The Apostle Paul declared in the Book of Corinthians that *I will let nothing separate me from the love of God not things, presents, nor things to come, nor principalities, or powers*! **(Romans 8:35).**

As I stated before, there cannot be any idolatry in our walk with God. We cannot place. anything in front of Him. God is a jealous God and all-consuming fire (Hebrews 12:29). We cannot even put our families before God if you do not believe me look at the life of Abraham in the Bible.

Abraham was tested by God to prove his love for Him when God asked him to bring his only son as an offering for the people. Abraham loved God so much that he carried his only son up on the mountain to kill him only to hear God say I was testing your obedience and love for me. He rewarded Abraham by providing him a sacrifice for the people! We know this is when Abraham's relationship with God shifted from his Heavenly Father to Jehovah Jireh, the God who provides for His children **(Genesis 22:14).**

We are living in a time where true love is scarcely sought after or seen among humanity and people are becoming more selfishly concerned for themselves. But the love of the Father does not just seek after its own but it covers a multitude of sins. *I am convinced until humanity* accepts the love of their Heavenly Father there will not be a full manifestation of the glory of God released on the earth. In Luke 10:2, ***"The harvest is plentiful but the laborers are few."*** There are very few Christians who will lay down their agenda for the cause of Christ for another life to be saved. At some point or another we have to face the question if I die today has my life counted for eternity? God wants pure vessels that He can use to fulfill His divine purpose for His children. When we say *"Daddy I Love You"* that means we are willing to go anywhere that He send us even it is to the uttermost parts of the earth. Jesus said, ***"If you love me, keep my commandments and I will leave you with a comforter who will lead you into all truth!"***

(St. John 14:15).

The word *love* is an action word and it carries an unconditional weight of God's glory. There will be times in all of our lives where God's love will test us in our obedience to do something that we have never done. Something that will cost us much but we will gain eternally and it will be a sacrifice. When we look at the life of the apostles especially the life of Paul their love for their daddy impacted the body of Christ, their communities, and the entire world. His encounter with God on the road to Damascus was a complete heart change in his life. God made his desires become His desires! In the early part of his life, he would not have anticipated becoming a leader for the Christian faith, he was heretic and one of the major persecutors of the *Church*. However, after God's love and light shined upon Him he accepted Christ in his life and the statement "Daddy I love You" became a sounding board to the church from Paul. His life was totally transformed. So now when you hear the words "DADDY I LOVE YOU" you no longer should interpret that to mean a cute phrase for a toddler to his earthly father but now we can see it in terms of giving our very lives away for the glory of God to be made manifest in the earth.

The Bible declares in Romans 8:19 (AMP) ***"That the earth groans and waits for the Sons of God to be manifested."*** Why? Because God needs you and me to reflect His love to humanity and He needs willing vessels that do not mind getting their hands dirty for

His work. When we do God's work we do not need recognition we should have a pure heart for what we do for Christ. Jesus said to His disciples, ***"The Heavens and earth will pass away but my Word will STAND"* (Luke 21:33).**

As I close this chapter, I would like you to say these words out of your mouth with a different attitude and believe that there is going to be a rapid transformation in your life when you say these words with all your heart "DADDY I LOVE YOU"

Something About the Name of Jesus

Did you know that the name Jesus is mentioned more than 900 times in the bible? **(www.whatchristianswanttoknow.com**, 1). *It is the only name given by God that we can be saved, for whoever calls on the name of Jesus shall be saved"* (Romans 10: 9-10, KJV). God has given His Son a name above every name that at the mention of His name bodies are healed, demons have to flee, and lives are forever changed. *Every knee shall bow, every tongue must confess that He is Lord (*Philippians 2:10**)** His name brings peace, His name brings joy, His name brings love, His name brings forgiveness, and reconciliation. When we pursue God, His name takes on another meaning. When we call on the name of Jesus, we do not call his name out of a mere ritual or cliché but we call Him out of a pure relationship with our Father. Have you ever been in trouble and you called on the name of Jesus and immediately whatever was happening ceased? I remember when I was driving to choir rehearsal and a car ran into the back of my vehicle and instantly my vehicle started spinning in the middle of the highway and when I called on the name of Jesus the car instantly stopped and faced the opposite direction on the highway.

There is power in the name of Jesus and as believers we have to understand the authority and power that we have in His name!

My purpose of writing this chapter is to make you aware that when you use the name of Jesus you will understand the full authority and power that comes with His name so you will not just use His name vicariously. Some Christians use His name vicariously because they do not have a relationship with God, nor do they pursue His heart. How would you feel if your son and daughter only called you on the phone when they needed something and not when they just wanted to speak with you? Jesus Christ wants us to be in relationship with Him daily and not just call on Him when we are in trouble. When Jesus chose His disciples, He chose men that would walk with Him and not just know about of Him. What is the difference between walking with someone and just knowing about them? When a person walks with you they have allotted the time to *Get to Know* you on a higher level so that when they call your name or when they hear your name it has a special meaning for them. In the same manner, when we walk with God when we use the name of Jesus or hear the name of Jesus it's not just a cliché to you but it has a special meaning for you because it comes out of your experience with Him.

    The world's idea of Jesus comes from a self-portrait of mass media sitcoms and movies such as *The Passion of Christ* neglecting the deeper meaning of the significance of having a relationship with Him. It's just not enough to know about God when you have the opportunity to sit at the table and eat with Him.

Our Savior longs to hear His name out of our mouth and those who call on the name of Jesus shall be saved! (Romans 10:13) His name is wonderful, His name is precious, His name is beautiful, His name is powerful, His name is _____. As I close this chapter you fill in the blank. I pray that every time you hear the name of Jesus or whenever the name of Jesus is mentioned you will meditate and reflect about the opportunity you have as His beloved children to speak well of His name, to make His name glorious in the earth, and most of all to sit down at His table and eat with Him.

My First Love

The Sound of Music is a Broadway musical emphasizing the union of a family and the father who meets a beautiful gifted woman and his children absolutely adore her! When I was little I always wondered why this movie was called "*The Sound of Music?*" In doing some research, I discovered that this movie was actually based on a true story and the housekeeper "Maria von Kutschera was once living as a novice until she met this man." **(www.panoramatours.com/sound, 1).** The broad way musical was named "The Sound of Music" in connection with a musical book called "*The Story of the Trapp Family Singers.*" In the beginning of the musical Maria was just keeping his children and then we see a shift taking place in their relationship. This man never knew that he had a hole in his heart until he met this lady. After he confessed his feelings for her we see the whole family take on a different persona! Likewise, when we yield to our Heavenly Father not only are we transformed but our entire families will be also.

As he got to know this young woman who seemed so intriguing to him he started to see her as more than just a housekeeper. Every day he anticipated spending time with her and we can see their love for one another when they sang to each other. Do you ever wonder why older people still watch this movie and cry like it was their first time watching it?

Could it be because they feel the soul stirring sincerity of innocent love? Ok, here goes my confession.... this is not a statistic yet that has been proven that I have researched but just voluntary and involuntary observations of this modern era. The innocence of love is not received in this era because we have been victimized and polluted to receive perverted love. What is perverted love? Perverted love is a form of love that is about power, prestige, position, money, lust, or any *chest game play*. If you are nice to someone with no evil intentions but to share the love of God with them people today think that you are weird, gay, or crazy!

There was a time when America embraced purity, the innocence of love, and most importantly God as the main attraction the morals of God! But now people are so distracted from their first love. Just think about it before there were any inventions, even before there was me and you, it was only God! But I am thoroughly convinced that God still has a faithful remnant who will be able to STAND because God's Word is infallible and He indicated in Paul's letter to the Corinthian Church that the greatest of these faith and hope was love. (1 Corinthians 13: hope, faith, charity).

Will You Return Back to Your First Love?
When we look at the Book of Hosea we should feel apathy and sympathy for this brother!

His wife is a prostitute and she has an inner craving to still be connected to the world however Hosea still loved his wife beyond her failures. No matter how many times his wife sinned against God, him, and the family, Hosea kept forgiving her just like our Heavenly Father forgives us. Did you know that there is no sin that you can commit that God is not willing to forgive accept blasphemy? Just like Hosea kept the door of his house open the door of our Heavenly Father is open to all. If you are reading this book and you know in your heart that you are still contemplating giving your life back to God take a quantum leap of faith and jump in the river! Return back to your first love. You know that feeling you once had when you dated the first boy or first girl. No one will ever forget the first person that they first dated I do not care what age you are that is just a special mark in that time of your life! I will never forget my first boyfriend Troy Engles because he was my first love and he gave me my first kiss. I hope that was not too much information but you get the gist of the message right. Nothing can replace the Heavenly Father in our lives. He gives the best kisses, the best hugs, and His love is unconditional! It is not based on merit, position, prestige, lust, His love is pure! Christ is my first love and I will never forget the moment that I fell in love with Him. That moment is something that I cannot describe. His love is the best that has ever been given and it's free to receive. You do not have to buy God's love. Can you believe that it's the best love and it does not even cost $1.00? That's too good to be true right? Naw, it's the real thing. Its real truth and you can experience it anytime. Ahavat Elohim means "The love of God. **For God *so loved the world that He gave His only begotten Son that whoever believes in Him will not ever die but will have everlasting life***" (John 3:16, AMP) As I close this chapter, please mediate on that Scripture and how much God loves you and the fact that it is the best love. Can God actually become your first love?

I believe that Jesus was a realist and one of the major reasons why the Pharisees rejected Him was because He was truthful concerning His purpose for being here on earth. He would say over and over again my meat is to do the will of the Father and the Spirit of the Lord is upon me for He has anointed me to bring the Gospel to the poor, to set at liberty, to give sight to the blind, to bring deliverance to all those who are oppressed (Luke 4:18). He was not here on earth to be a part of any cliques or social parties. His mission was to share the love of His Father to all people and win souls for the Kingdom of God. When I think about the love of God it reminds me of a hymn called *"The Blood Song"* that we sing at church often during communion. His blood does reach to the highest mountain and it will flow to the lowest valley, the blood that Jesus shed will never lose its power. I truly thank God that the blood of Jesus will never lose its power!

His love is so great for you and me that it supersedes all our doubts, all our fears, and all legalities. God's love does not show respect of person and what He has done for me He can do for you! Regardless of what road you have been on before when you come in contact with the one true and living God your life will never be the same. His love is that strong, His love is that wide, His love is that deep, and His love is that solid! Christ's love is like a rock you can count on it and it will always be there no matter where in life you find yourself positioned.

As I close this chapter, I would like you to meditate on how the love of God has been there for you the Ahavat Elohim' and write a love-letter back to God and read it to Him aloud. And if you have fallen astray and you would like to re-commit to your first love, just tell Him. He's waiting for you with open arms to receive you as His son or daughter! **(Luke 15:20).**

I Won't Go Back

How many times do we say to ourselves that after we have encountered a bad relationship that we will not go back to that man or woman? Especially a woman being battered by her boyfriend or an unfaithful spouse, we find ourselves saying these words I WON'T GO BACK! About 4,000 women die each year due to domestic violence. On average, a woman will leave an abusive relationship seven times before she leaves for good www.clarkprosecutor.org, but it has also been proven that Christian believers who have healthy support groups and counselors do not return back to their same lifestyle. (**www.vawnet.org, 1**). They can survive with the advice that they receive from their peer groups and counselor.
(**www.thehotline.org./add, 1**).

Remember when Jesus healed the ten lepers He told them *"Go and Sin No More."* In the same manner, in our walk with God we have to set boundaries around our personal relationships and who we allow in our *inner circle*. We should always be led by the Holy Spirit about who we connect with on an everyday basis and if it causes us to digress in our relationship with the Lord then we have to pray for that person and love them from a distance.

As you read this chapter, I pray that the Holy Spirit will sharpen your discernment and as you pursue the Lord with all your heart, your strength, your mind, and your soul that He would quicken your spirit to check your house. Check to see if there are any areas that the enemy has crept into your life to cause you to live in bondage or live a life of oppression. Romans 12:2 says *"**Do not be conformed to this world but be transformed by the renewing of your mind. Then you will be able to discern the will of God, what is good and acceptable and perfect.**"* In order for you to stay free and not to return to bondage you have to renew your mind with the word of God every day. You have to eat the Word just like you feed your stomach and be open to tell God your vulnerabilities. Please allow the Holy Spirit to be your guide to help you discern what is evil from what is good in your relationships (John 16:12; 2 Corn. 6:14-18; Galatians 5:22). In this process, you will confront a term called *repudiate,* it means to refuse to be associated and to separate.

In our pursuit of God, we have to totally repudiate from every ungodly relationship that pulls us away from God's call on our lives or that tries to kill us. We have to remove ourselves from the entire situation in order to move forward. Just know that you're not a failure in this process. It's not your fault and God is calling for you to *Break Out*!

Break Out!
There is nothing to be afraid of because the Bible explicitly says only fear God do not fear man He is the one who holds your key to Heaven's door. Knock, knock, knock, God is calling you.

Will you answer Him? Will you be the one willing to come from among the crowd? He is the one who holds your destiny, not man! It's time to break out. Break out even if it is your church that is holding you captive, even if it is your relationship, your job, your family. Whatever it is, it is time for YOU to *Break Out*. Do not let anything or anyone hold you back! Your time is now, so choose, to follow the leading of the Holy Spirit. Paul said, "***Forgetting those things behind me, reaching out towards those things in front of me I press toward the mark of the high calling in Jesus Christ***" (Philippians 3:14). "*If God be for you, who can be against you*" **(Romans 8:31).** Please know that He who began a good work in you is faithful to complete that work until the return of Jesus Christ **(Philippians 1:6).**

As I close this chapter, I challenge you to confess the words that are below and to "Break Out" from all toxic relationships that are killing your passion for God.

Confession

I am an overcomer by the blood of the Lamb and by the word of my testimony and I won't go back to the way things used to be. The old ways that consumed me and my past no longer dictate my future. I live a life that has been totally transformed by the power of God and in the name of Jesus. My life is aligned with the word of God and every stronghold, every generational curse, every diabolical plan of the enemy has been cursed at the root, and stopped by the blood of Jesus. I am now a transformed person through the Holy Spirit and I am walking and pursuing my Abba father (my daddy) and His mandate on my life! My mind is renewed, my spirit is restored, and I am healed totally by the stripes of Jesus. God I decree and declare that I WON'T GO BACK.

Yeshua!

Jesus is My Rescuer & My deliverer!
At age 17, Yeshua' totally transformed my life when I totally surrendered to the call of God on my life. I was so desperate in that season for God to love me and show me more that He could do in my life. Before this happened, I was so empty and sometimes I found myself suicidal because of so much verbal abuse I faced every day at school. As a teenager, it affected my self-esteem. I thank God for my parents who spoke positive words over my life. Those words they gave me power to "live." Whether we realize it or not the words we speak over our children have power. In the book of James, he tells us to guard our mouths to only speak the word of God. Even Paul said that, ***"The Lord gave me strength so that through me the message might be fully proclaimed and all the Gentiles might hear it"* (2 Timothy 4:17).** Paul was rescued by Yeshua from the snares of the enemy **(1 Timothy 4:1)**. The Lord will also rescue us all from every evil attack of our adversary and save us so that our Heavenly assignment will be fulfilled!

My Love Letter to Yeshua
Hello Dad! I thank you for being my best-friend, my lover, and my Lord. There were times that I could have given up in my life but you have made me become more than a conqueror in you!

I held on to your Word and you did not let me fall. I thank you that your plan and purpose have prevailed in my life and caused me to STAND. Thank you for these last two years that I have seen so many miracles take place in my life and now you have made me become a testimony to the world that you may get the glory and honor. I live for you Yeshua and I am so in love with you God! This morning when I woke up I was so excited because my life in you has taken a different course just because I said Yes! Lord I want you more than anything. I do not want money, I do not want fame, I just want you and to do your will. Thank you for loving me with agape love (love in its most-purest form). You just want my worship, my obedience, my service, my love, and I am your vessel. You have helped me defeat all of my giants! I can stay in your presence forever! Yeshua, you are the MAN! I will wait before making any other move, you tell me and I am open to hear from you God. I love you Yeshua!'

Your daughter,
Monique Lewis

I Almost Let Go

'I waited for a long time to hear from you and then the phone rang and I anticipated to hear your voice, but when I answered the phone it was someone else on the other line." Have you ever experienced being so in love with your boyfriend or girlfriend that every time the phone rang your heart-skipped a beat because you thought it might be him? I wonder what would happen if we had that same anticipation and hunger for God in our lives. There would be no need for the excessive texting on our cell-phones or playing with applications anymore. I remember when I was little girl my father used to forbid me from talking to guys on the phone until I was 15 years old. I would be so upset. My first real-love who I mentioned before Troy Eggleton would tell me, "Monique I keep calling you and your father keeps hanging up on me!" (LOL) *Aren't you glad that our Heavenly Father never hangs the phone up on us when we call on Him*? But the truth of the matter is that in our pursuit of God we all face a breaking point where we get to the place of birth the canal is opened and we stop believing God. At this present moment, as I am writing this book I have just experienced a **"PUSH THROUGH MOMENT!"** PUSH: Pray, Until, Something, Happens. I refuse to let go because there is something on the inside of me that keeps pushing me toward my purpose.

Regardless of my natural circumstances I still believe God and no one can convince me that God is not working on my behalf! By the grace of God I just signed my first recording contract with Tate Music Group and I am super-excited! Yes, I am a living testimony that you can walk on the water alone just keep the faith.

Even Jesus told Peter to come out of the boat and walk on the water with Him. He specifically asked him *only* and this is very significant for us to realize today. Why? Peter teaches us to have the courage and to not be afraid of stepping into unfamiliar territory. God is our compass and in Him we find our roadmap. We just respond by being obedient to His commands. So, I encourage you as you are reading this book to know that God has a predestinated purpose for your life and He loves you more than you could ever imagine. Please do not give up, regardless of how your situation looks know that God ultimately wants to be glorified! ***Weeping may endure for a night, but joy is coming in the morning*** (Psalm 30:5). Although you may be facing an illness, a divorce, a child's death, a parent's death, a job loss, or a financial dilemma GOD IS IN CONTROL. ***"Lift your eyes up to Heaven for all your help comes from the Lord. He will not allow your foot to slip or to be moved; He who keeps you will not slumber. The Lord is your keeper, the Lord is your shade on your right hand, the sun shall not smite you by day or night.***

The Lord will keep you from all evil; He will keep your life." (Psalm 123:1-5, AMP).

No More Fear

Packing can be quite liberating especially when you are going on vacation but the problem comes when we want to carry everything that we own in our personal luggage. For some of us it takes at least a half of a day to pack while others it may take only a few hours. However, the fact remains that packing is a PROCESS and in the time, we are living in now you do not want to be over-loaded. Believe me when I say that the airlines will charge you an extra 25.00-75.00$ at the check-in line and we have seen that happen over and over again while checking our own bags in preparation for boarding the plane. May I ask you this question…what are you carrying in your luggage today? What are you carrying that needs to be sorted out or even thrown away? You may have some dirty laundry that needs to be washed, hung up, and air-dried. Whatever it is you cannot take all of your excessive baggage on the plane with you. I believe one of the hardest decisions for us in life is getting rid of the old and embracing the new. Even when it entails us sorting things out of our daily closets we hold on to the memories of those clothes, who gave us those clothes, and the seasons that we were living in our lives. Rick bought me these beautiful shoes when we were dating and I absolutely love these shoes and I cannot even grasp the thought of giving them away.

This is just an example of sometimes how *"we"* think as it relates to gifts; these are my shoes don't touch them. These are my clothes don't touch them, that's my necklace don't touch it, and etc. There is a fear of letting go of the past that haunts us when we are clinging to those precious moments. My challenge for you is to confront the fear of letting go of your past. It may initially begin with you sorting out your closet. Ask yourself the question what needs to remain or what do I need to give away or throw in the garbage bin? Because we all have to understand if our closets are full of old garments we cannot make room for the new garments (Mark 2:21).

When we look at our closets we should see a certain picture unfolding that reveals to us the essence of who He has called us to be as citizens of His Kingdom. In our lives, we have to get to the place where we have no more fear of the past because one truth that remains evident is that you cannot change your past. I would like to add to this statement. I am not ashamed of my past and you should not be ashamed of yours either! Our past has been re-written by our Savior Jesus Christ and *He paid it all*! We do not have to prove ourselves to anyone or anything, just share the love of Jesus Christ to all people. When you let go and let God you will embrace and embark on a new you, the unique you, who you were created to be when God breathed upon man from the dust of the earth and man became a living soul! (Genesis 1:27).

I challenge you to walk in the power and the authority of God and take your rightful position as a citizen of Heaven with *no baggage to claim but only what God has ordained*! For God, has not given you the spirit of fear but of power, love, and of a sound mind (2 Timothy: 1). As I close this chapter, I challenge you today to say your final GOODBYE to FEAR!

ZOE "The Life"

Since we are made in the imago dei of God, God has orchestrated us with new magnesium for His purpose for our lives. The breath of God that came from His nostrils when He breathed into man and maximized his potential. Just like an atomic neutron plays it's role within its family unit when you entered into the family of God you became part of a new *Life and a new atomic bomb!* It is in that place when you realize who you are in God and where your new life begins to unfold. Living beyond the norm of the natural man and his acclaimed intelligence or superficial self-imposed identity. True living means self–denial. I give myself away is one of the most powerful worship songs. Written by William Mcdowell, it reveals the authenticity of the character and very nature of God. We should not always have the perspective of what God can do for us but what we can do for Him. God's command was to multiply Himself in the earth through you and me! He said, **"Be Fruitful and multiply"** (Genesis 1:28). The *Zoe (Life)* is redeeming man back to His rightful place of pursuing Him for Heaven's dominion and fulfilling your God ordained assignment!

People may not be aware of the times and seasons that we are living in today but we are in the era of Noah. In that time in the world the people were living in rebellion, walking in darkness, and worshiping gods other than Jehovah.

But look at the text and its entirety God said if "**He finds fifty righteous then I will spare the people and He found one and that was Noah and he told him to prepare the ark to be a refuge for the people**" (Genesis 18:26). The people laughed at Him and they mocked Him because they did not believe that God would destroy the land. God told Noah to save his family and his livestock and when the flood came, God commanded Him to shut the door and the people who mocked at Him could not enter in the ark. What does the ark represent today? Who are the Noahs today? Who will have the courage to be set a part, to be different and to take a leap of faith? At this present moment, I have seen another revelation that I probably would not have received four years ago. The Bible says, *"Our obedience is better than sacrifice"* (Samuel 15:22). Oftentimes in life we have to be still, be patient, and wait for all the instructions from God. Being still does not mean that you are rebelling against God but that you are waiting and allowing him to change your way of living.

For the love of money is the root of all evil. Life is not about how many *things* that you possess because whatever you have it all belongs to Him. I thank God for the decisions that I have made so far in my life. They are decisions by the Holy Spirit and now it has been revealed to me what a *"refuge"* really means! It is the place of safety, the place of God's presence, and His protection over you. God told me not to go back to work in the secular world but He was going to open doors for me musically this year and He has. Now it's time to make this next decision for where I will serve since I have served my local church faithfully for 31 years. My assignment has come to an end. This was revealed to me by the Spirit of the Lord and I have been praying concerning the place God has for me. I have been crying out to the Lord for clarity. I will miss my pastor and I know that I will miss the people. God has literally changed my life and I know that my music ministry is being birthed, songs from the heart of God. It is time so I say this with every breath of my body God You HAVE ALL OF ME! I will continually serve in my community. I know that this is just the beginning. GOD HAS LITERALLY CHANGED MY LIFE!!! I have chosen to obey and I continue to pray for clarity on what door it is to spiritually minister to my spirit.

Stop in the Name of Love

Stop in the Name of Love
We thank God for Kellogg's Cornflakes, Fruit-Loops, Chef Boyardee, and Tyson's Chicken Nuggets but the greatest brand we could ever endorse is "OUR GOD: THE GREAT I AM!" In the world, we live in today so many people are searching to find that love, that joy, that peace, in people, places, and things. But if they would just stop and receive the true agape love of God they would quickly come to the realization that there is no one > than our GOD. I was driving down the highway and the Lord reminded me in a still small voice and said these words, ***"Monique do not make your next decision for your musical assignment based on people, places, or things but by the Spirit of God."***

In our pursuit of God and oftentimes in our journey we have to know the power in the word STOP! If you keep moving while in transition instead of being still until you get clear direction you could actually have a train wreck on your journey. When our minds are completely transformed by the Spirit of the Lord we know how to fully operate in the kingdom and we no longer question or worry about the outcome because God has already established His stamp of approval for success! The old-school song entitled "***Stop in the name of love before you break my heart,***" is a secular song but the words have so much meaning behind them.

When you are in love with God just like you are in love with your spouse, or boyfriend, or girlfriend the relationship has its set course and its set rhythm just like a drum., There are times when the drummer has to stop for breaks in the song and then pick the rhythm back up in the chorus. There has to be a clear wave of understanding between the band and the artist. In the same manner, in our relationship with God and His people there has to be a mutual understanding. When God is speaking, we have to be silent. We have to stop and listen so that we can move to our next dimension in Him! So, I beg you out of all the sirens, the family issues, the financial issues that you may be facing take a moment to STOP in the name of your love for Jesus Christ and don't make another move until you hear His voice. Sometimes God is testing your faith to see if you will keep pursuing Him even in your darkest moments!

Knock, Knock, Knock, It's Me Again....

Time plays a very significant role in every human being's life. Ecclesiastes 3:1 says, *"To everything there is a season and a time to every purpose under the Heaven."* How do you govern your time? As you read this chapter, I would like you to ponder on how much time you give God in every area of your life because He is standing at the door knocking waiting for you to answer His call. As we continue to develop and learn in our pursuit of God we cannot help but see the real purpose of why we were created on earth and given keys to His Kingdom. While others think that their purpose in life is just to have a Mercedes Ben, a retirement fund, and lavish homes God is saying what about me? Are you adhering to my purpose for your life and what I have called you to do? Please do not misunderstand me. We all want to be endowed with His blessings because they do make us rich and add no sorrow but do not neglect your Creator. Make time for God. It is very pertinent in our lives to hear God and obey him beyond our natural cravings for fleshly things to feel affirmed or validated as Believers. So many people put themselves in dangerous positions to acquire the *American Dream* instead of standing on Matthew 6:33 that says, *"Seek ye first the Kingdom of God and all of His righteousness and all of these things will be added unto you."*

We have to know who we are in God so much that we are captivated to another level in our walk with God and understand our Heavenly Assignment. We should never waste our time! It is a dishonor and a disgrace to God and to His people. Some of our schedules may look like this:

8:00 am: Go to Work
12:00 pm: Go to Lunch
5:00pm: Get off Work
6:00pm: Cook Dinner
7:00: Family Time
9:00pm: Go to Bed

When do we make time for God? Because God never intended for His people to live by daily rituals and not really know what it means to live in the Kingdom of God. Every day we should pray on how God wants us to govern our day that He may be glorified and pleased. It is important that we take personal responsibility and ownership about who we are connected to be it our relationships, church, businesses, or job because if they are not connected to our destiny we are wasting our time. I challenge you today to give your time back to God and to not always come to Him with your hands out like He's your "sugar-daddy." When you trust the Lord the Bible declares that *"**His favor will compass you like a shield and you will have favor with God and man**"* (Psalm 5:12). As I am writing this book, I want to declare to you while lying on this bed that I know without a shadow of doubt that I will be a millionaire and it is not just because I work hard but because I have given my life totally to the pursuit of God. You can work hard *all day* and still not please God! The Bible says, unless "***God builds a house their labor will be in vain***" (Psalm 127:1). Jesus gave us the keys to His Kingdom and the wisdom of God is far above rubies and I understand that at a greater level now (Matthew 16:19).

What Does It Mean To Be In The Will of God?

When you are in the will of God you will have peace, overflowing joy, love, and most of all God's anointing on your assignment. Again, Jesus understood His assignment when he quoted the prophet Isaiah and said "**The spirit of the Lord is upon me for He has anointed me to preach the Gospel to the poor, he has sent me to proclaim freedom for the prisoners, to heal those who are blind, and to set the oppressed free**" (Luke 4:18). It is imperative that we recognize who Christ is, His purpose for our life, and then commit to doing His will. Jesus has always committed himself to do the will of God and he is an example for us today. When He was twelve years old, he was in the temple teaching and his parents could not find him. He said, ***"Who is my mother and father, they are my mother father, this is my family!***

(Matthew 12:48) This gives us the revelation that as faithful servants of God you serve God's people just like you are serving your own flesh and blood. This does not mean that he would neglect his parents for doing the will of God it just means that his obedience required Him to serve on a greater level. As Christian believers, we have to also see ourselves in the future and be very prayerful concerning who we marry, who our friends are, who we mentor, who we allow to mentor us, who we share our visions with, who we give access to, and what job or career we embark upon. Again, when you are in the will of God you will have peace, overflowing joy, love, and most all God's anointing on your assignment.

When you make time for God He will show you how to invest your money, where to put your name on the dotted line, how to get out of financial troubles, when to buy and when to save your money. I have to admit previously in my twenties I did not understand that concept so I just thought you just worked hard to earn money and then you inherited the finer things in life. At that time in my life I did not understand how your career is related to your purpose. But now I understand the importance of seeking God's face, God's hand, God's heart, and God's will. In our life journey, to be effective witnesses and fulfill the mantel of God on our lives we have to zealously pursue God by living a lifestyle of prayer. Kneeling before His throne because His will is good and His will is perfect!

He's knocking at your door will you answer Him? **(Matthew 7:7)** He is waiting for your response. I challenge you to open the door by speaking back to him. Have a conversation with your Father?

Seeking the Heart of God

I would like to start this chapter by saying that the heart of God is only revealed to believers who hunger and thirst after righteousness (Matthew 5:6). Do you know what it means to be filled as a *believer*? When we pursue God, we are filled with not only His Word, but we are also infused with the endowment of the Holy Spirit and we begin to hear the heart-beat of God! Just listen…. thump…. thump…. thump…. thump…. thump… thump…. thump…. As you are listening to God's heart-beat? Please meditate on this beautiful song and pay close attention to the lyrics below as you are listening in the Spirit to the heart-beat of God.

As the Deer

By Martin J. Nystrom

As the deer panteth for the water
So my soul longeth after You
You alone are my heart's desire
And I long to worship You

You alone are my strength, my shield
To You alone may my spirit yield
You alone are my heart's desire
And I long to worship You

You're my friend and You are my brother
Even though You are a king
And I love You more than any other

So much more than anything

Chorus

I want You more than gold or silver
Only You can satisfy
You alone are the real joy giver
And the apple of my eye

(Psalm 42:1)

The songwriter pinned "My soul longs for you just like a deer yearns for water." When we worship God, there is a desire that we have to feel His presence and to hear His heartbeat. God what do you have to say to me? What is in on your mind? We have to be open to hear what God has to say about others and not just about us or our own situations.

When you hear the heart-beat of God you no longer ignore the cry of innocent children being raped, single-mothers who cannot afford to pay for diapers in the grocery store, babies who are dying of hunger, the mail man who just lost his job, and the homeless living on the street, or you hear the cries of prisoners who are begging for one more chance to re-live that moment and make the right choice, or the human-trafficking victims who are enslaved by injustices. Can you hear their cries? Can you hear the heart of God and what is on His shoulder?

Sometimes I hear the cries so much in my spirit that it literally drives me with passion to finish everything God has assigned me to do like go back to school so that I can develop all these programs that are locked up on the inside of me.

I cannot die without fulfilling the call of God on my life I know that it is very imperative that I finish my course just like the Apostle Paul stated in the New Testament (2 Timothy 4:7). When you began to hear the heart-beat of God it's no longer about you and your life but it becomes about Him and others! *The heart of God compels us to take action*! It is about fighting against racial injustice and so many disadvantages that have happened today to our children. There are children who do not have a voice and their lives are at risk. Will you speak for them? I remember when I went to Haiti. The first day we had bubbles and some candy with us but as I observed the kids I could not help but notice that they were coming around us like they rarely ever had the opportunity to play with bubbles or eat candy. In comparison to the children in America, our children would have iPads, television, satellites (Direct TV) cell phones, the Wii games and much more for entertainment and sometimes they are still not satisfied. Will the real Church wake up? We are sleeping and we do not even realize it. God needs you and me to be beacons of light to the world. Some of us who live in America have been so spoiled by life's gadgets that we are no longer pursuing the heart of God.

According to Michael Lipka, "Only 37 percent of their membership are present for the average Sunday morning worship service" (**www.pewresearch.org**, 1). We are no longer attending church because we are distracted by life's gadgets and church is not a part of our "To Do List."

God's Heart for the Nations

Every day at Global Leadership Training Center we would pray this prayer. Ask and I will give the nations to you says the Lord! That is the cry of God's heart for you and me to bring God's healing power to the ends of the earth!

Isaiah 66:1 (KJV) says, ***"The heaven's is my throne, and the earth is my footstool: where is the house that ye build unto me? And where is the place of my rest? For all those things hath mine hand made, and all those things have been, saith the Lord; but to this man will I look even to him that is poor and of a contrite spirit, and trembled at my word."***

Can you hear the sound? The sound of the nation's calling you? Will you go or who will you send? I never knew at the age of 30 that I would ever go to the mission's field. I remember when all of my friends at ORU use to go and I would support them but deep inside I could never imagine myself on the mission's field. At that moment, I had not really heard God to be a goer for missions.

It was not until the summer of 2009 when I was in prayer (I shared this previously with you) when I woke up that I knew that God was preparing me to be a "goer" and I told my spiritual father. During that same year, I kept seeing a vision of young people singing and I saw a stage and that's when in my spirit the name came SOULED OUT. I knew it was an outreach but I had no knowledge of how this was going to be executed nor how to create an outreach beyond our American borders. So, I just continued to pray and I will never forget the moment I met a missionary at Tulsa International Airport. My spirit leaped and before I knew it I found myself telling her about an outreach God told me to do and she told me about going to my first missions trip with Cruise for a Cause.

In addition to this, I saw that she had a school for Global leadership on her website and my spirit was really leaping now because I was thinking this would really help me become more equipped to start this outreach. So, I called the school. One of the pastors was so nice she gave me all the information that I needed to know to attend the school and I said to myself at that moment, God I do not have the money to attend this program so I am just going to save for next semester. Did I have faith? I think I did but I was praying hard that I get the money for next semester. This is one of the moments when the favor of God just takes over your life because it absolutely could not be denied. When I turned around not only was I a student learning about the nations and the call God had on my life but I became a true spiritual daughter. I am so grateful to the Lord and I give Him all glory. Now Youth in Christ Souled-Out will be launched and will not only be a blessing to the community, cities and to the nations but it will also be a blessing to several ministries. I cannot believe this all began when I said yes to the heartbeat of God and agreed to go to the nations of the earth. Can you hear God's heartbeat and will you go? I am a true witness that your yes to God will be your faith that unlocks the door to your destiny! You will not have to question God on how, when, where, why, who, or what but His will shall be done! My challenge is for you to spend some quiet time before the Lord today and actually listen to hear God's heartbeat. Take your journal and write down what God says to you.

You Go Girl

Today as I am writing to you it is September 11, 2012, the historical tragic day when the twin towers of New York were hit by terrorists and I am taking a moment of silence in remembrance for the families who may have lost their loved ones:

Dear God, the God of all comfort, please shine your peace down on those who are facing a difficult time right now. Send your angelic host and surround them with your grace. Now may the peace of God that passes all understanding guard their hearts and minds through Christ Jesus. Amen.

As I begin this chapter, it is very significant that we understand that the word *Go* is an action verb to direct us to our next destination in God. Repeatedly we ask ourselves this question in our faith journey, 0what is next God? What do you see on the next page of my life? Well we won't know unless we make the decision to turn the page. Have you ever been afraid to turn the page? There was a time previously in my life that I used to be afraid of turning the page but not anymore because of the hope of glory that lives on the inside of me. On August 25, 2012, I stepped totally out on faith in obedience to God and officially had the first meeting for Youth in Christ. The meeting was so amazing and I thank God for all that He is doing and it is marvelous.

We have a huge event coming up very soon and I BELIEVE GOD IS GOING TO DO EVEN MORE! I am very prayerful during these events and meetings. On last Saturday, I had another meeting that went well with one of the moderators of our faith and I was blown away! I am so grateful that God is making the way clear and prospering everything that we put our hands to do for His Kingdom.

Yes, I am a true witness that when we start to turn the page and trust God our lives begin to take the road that is less traveled. It is the road that very few people will find because it's very narrow (Robert Frost, 1). On this road, we no longer worry about the cares of this world and run after fame or fortune but we *run* towards God. Whitney Houston sung a song that says *"I want to run to you"* that speaks of the passion we have as women towards the men in our life. Sometimes you are so in love with your Boaz that you cannot wait until he gets off work. If you take that same passion towards the Lord you will see that **"No good thing will He withhold to those who walk upright!"** (Psalm 84:11). When you love God and are faithful to His assignment you are not easily moved by the crowd or what others may think. *You* become a leader and you are confident in who you are in God.

In the Gospel of Matthew 28: 18-20, Jesus emphasizes the Great Commission to the body of Christ to **"Go into all the world and make disciples**

baptizing them in the Father, the Son, and the Holy Spirit." He assures us that God will be with us always while we are working in His vineyard. To fulfill the Great Commission, it requires a serious commitment to the Lord that cannot be taken as religious jargon or a pious gesture. There are people who do pious acts all over this country for several charitable organizations but that does not mean that they are fulfilling the Great Commission (James 1:26). It is the body of Christ's responsibility to witness the Gospel by feeding the hungry, clothing the naked, visiting the sick, ministering to the prisoners, giving people water when they are thirsty, and to be willing to open our homes as a safe haven to help others who are in need. By doing this God is pleased because we have helped the *least of these*. Christianity is visiting the fatherless and widows in their affliction and to keep yourself unspotted from the world (James 1: 27). In a world that is full of chaos and evil there is still hope because God has you and me! I made a conscious decision to not ***allow anything to separate me from my love for God, nothing present, nor things to come***, can keep me from pursuing God and His assignment on my life. What about you? You should no longer allow the things of this present world to pull you away from fulfilling the Great Commission or dictate your future. Again, Paul said, ***"Forget those things that are behind you and run towards those things that are in front of you"*** and begin to press towards the pursuit of God! *For it is the mark of the high calling of Jesus Christ* (Philippians 3:13). You "Go" and fulfill His mandate. Please know that God has already begun a good work in you and He is faithful to complete it until Christ returns.

I challenge you today to *Go* by taking action; Put the torch in your hand and turn the page. In life, we have to sometimes see ourselves like children in a race and when the coach says "On your Mark, Get Set, and Go" we have to run to God and answer the call He has upon our lives!

It's About You

Did you know that the greatest masterpiece that God has ever made was when He created you? You are fearfully and wonderfully made! (Psalm 139:14). But learning to embrace who you are in God is one of the greatest challenges for many Christians. At the end of the day, God is looking at you and declaring to you that you are the apple in His eye. You are an original and the moment you begin to embrace that is when you will begin to fall down on our knees and cry *"Holy, Holy, Holy thou art Holy"* (Isaiah 6:3) There is no one on earth besides God who can distinguish every fingerprint of His creation! (He has counted every hair that is on your head)

We have made the choice to follow Jesus and run hard after Him! The more I embrace who I am the more He reveals more to you! You need to know that God has given you all authority and power to possess His Kingdom promises. When God made us, He created man to reveal His glory, His light, and in return we manifest that (same) light towards Him. Jesus said it best speaking to the disciples, ***"No one takes a bushel and covers the light, instead the light is open for all to see"*** (Matthew 5:15).

In the same manner, the enemy tries to manipulate us by holding us captive by fear, intimidation, doubt, insecurity, hopelessness, addictions, self-abuse and unhealthy relationships. He wants to kill that light or that glory on the inside of us.

But we have the strength of God to combat His plan and walk in the light of God! It's time to embrace all that God has put in you before the foundations of the world and put on the whole armor of God so that you can stand against the wiles of the devil! It is "You" who God is calling! It is "You" who He needs to stand in the gap, It is "You" who He needs to be in that secret place, It is "You" who will lead the Israelites out of the wilderness and into the place of their promise. God needs you to embrace who He is on the inside of you!

Although we work, worship, and reside with hundreds of people every day God sees beyond the crowd and like a microscope is dissecting each part of the sample. He is watching you! But He is not watching to find the wrong in your life, He is looking for His glory to be made manifest in your life. Why? Because at the end of the day "It is about you" so embrace who you are in God and step-up to the assignment that He is calling you to do!

My Heart is Crying

Thump, Thump, Thump. Can you hear my heart-beat crying from the wilderness? The wilderness is a dry place for anything or anyone to live. The cry of the heart is when you are aching with pain and hurt from dealing with the issues of life. The Bible tells us to ***"Guard our heart with all diligence for out of it will flow the issues of life." (Proverbs 4:23)*** How do you guard your heart when it is still bleeding on the inside? Your mind is wondering *does God still love me?* Has He abandoned me? The cry of the heart will at times make you question the very existence of God and His grace on your life. But you have to remember that David said, ***"Hear my cry oh lord, incline to hear my request"*** Psalm 61:1) Even when we are in the desert God will be a present help in the time of our trouble (transition). Although our heart is aching we know that God will turn every bad situation for a greater destination.

In spite of it all, choose to live and not die so that you can declare the works of the Lord! (Psalm 118:17). "You are a winner and not a loser, you are chosen to overcome, you have been called for greatness, you are a winner and you will overcome!" Written by Monique Lewis. The cry of the heart is something that we share with others we feel comfortable with or those who can relate to our pain. But it is in the cry of the heart that we become broken so that God can use us.

Before the clay is put on the potter's wheel it is first beat, sprinkled with water, and then put on the wheel for further shaping until it comes to the *design of the artist* (Isaiah 64:8). If you are reading this book and you have a cry in your heart please know God can heal every pain that you are feeling. I would like to share with you a new worship song that the Lord gave me about the grace of God. Please meditate on the lyrics in this song.

Before the clay is put on the potter's wheel it is first beat, sprinkled with water, and then put on the wheel for further shaping until it comes to the *design of the artist* (Isaiah 64:8). If you are reading this book and you have a cry in your heart, please know God can heal every pain that you are feeling. I would like to share with you a new worship song that the Lord gave me about the grace of God. Please meditate on the lyrics in this song.

"It's all about You"
It's all about You Jesus
You are the reason why I live
You are the reason why I give
"Repeat"
"It's all about You"
And my life is a testimony
Of how your love and grace
Never failed me

Seeking the Face of God

Every morning our day should begin with prayer. We should always put God first in our lives and give him the honor that He deserves. Proverbs 1:7 says, that the ***"Fear of the Lord is the beginning of wisdom."*** We can see in the world that we live in today that we need God more than the air we breathe. In the last days, Paul tells us that people will be cold-hearted and will be lovers of themselves; doing all kinds of evil to one another (2 Timothy: 3). In order to combat the schemes of the enemy we have to pray to God on a consistent basis asking him to heal our land. 2 Chronicles 7:14 says, ***"If my people who are called by name will humble themselves and pray seek my face and turn from their wicked ways then will I hear from Heaven and heal their land."*** Most of the time, we do not realize that the healing that we need requires us to seek God more in our prayer life. But we have to **"Seek Him while He may be found and call upon Him while He is near"** (Isaiah 55:6).

Most of the prophets received their instructions from God through prayer and intercession. Daniel prayed three times a day in the city of Babylon despite the rules or laws of a land that was filled with idolatry, witchcraft, rebellion, and seducing spirits. He sought the face of God for deliverance for the people of the land to come into the knowledge of who the true and living God was Jehovah (The Great I am).

As a result, King Nebuchadnezzar and the people were able to see who the Triune God was and they began to acknowledge that He was the true and living God. It was Daniel who received prophetic visions and dreams from God about what was happening for the present and what was to come in the future. He also received the gift of interpreting the King's dreams because He was seeking the face of God on a consistent basis. Do you seek God for things or do you seek God's face for His instructions? We have to understand that every opportunity that we get to pray is vital to our destiny and others! We should seek God's face not just for ourselves but on the behalf of others. Christ was not selfish, He gave all He had on the cross so that all may come to know who He is and that He wants everyone to have a better way.

Hannah was another prayer warrior that sought the face of God in the midst of adversity and humiliation. For several years, Hannah prayed to God for a baby that she promised to give back to God. During this time women were not valued by their occupation but primarily by their seed (children). If a woman did not bear children it was a disgrace to her husband and her entire family. Hannah who at one time could not bear a child was mocked and treated harshly within her culture. But God heard her cry and granted her request and Hannah had a son named Samuel who began to be the prophet to the nation of Israel. Can you believe that Hannah was 130 years when God finally opened up her womb?

She is an encouragement to continue to pray even when the odds are against you. God has the power over the doctor's prognosis don't stop praying! The Bible indicates that when Hannah prayed that she cried out to the Lord so long that she began to get drunk in her spirit. When Eli the priest saw her in the temple praying he mistakenly thought that she was intoxicated (1Samuel 2).

We have to stay connected to the right power line (source) by putting God first through prayer. The only way we can operate in our full capacity and receive all that God has given us is to tap into the true power line that can release Heaven's will down on earth. For whatever we lose through our prayer life in Heaven shall be loosed on earth. *__Whatever we bind through our prayer from earth shall be bound also in Heaven__* (Matthew 18:18) Please do not underestimate the power that God has given you through His Word that He has placed in your mouth.

Job 22:28 **says,** *"You shall also decree a thing, and it shall be established unto thee, you shall form a purpose or plan, and it shall not be frustrated. It shall not be opposed by the events of divine providence, but whatever you undertake shall prosper. And the light shall shine upon thy ways you shall be prospered in all things, instead of being overtaken by calamity."*

In the book of Acts in chapter 4, we see another power example of the power of prayer and intercession among the early church on behalf of Peter and John who were wrongfully thrown into prison for sharing the Gospel in the community. They prayed for boldness and for the situation to be rectified. After hearing the accusations (the church) ***"They raised their voices together to God and said Sovereign Lord who made the heaven and the earth, the sea and everything in them it is in you who said by the Holy Spirit and they spoke the Word with boldness"*** (Acts 4:24). As a result, Peter and John were released and there was a greater sense of unity among the body of Christ. No one claimed that what they had was their own but they shared their possessions. Prayer is the primary tool used to fight against strongholds that try to plague our churches, families, and our individual lives.

Seeking the face of God will help us to continually live in the Spirit and not seek after the flesh (Galatians 5:16). As we seek God's face we will see the layers of our old nature begin to be peeled off of us as the new nature of the Holy Spirit begins to take control of our lives. The Book of James gives us insight on how to control our tongues through the word of God he said ***"Bitter and sweet water cannot flow together"*** (James 3:11). As we discipline ourselves by studying the word of God and through prayer we can truly start to live out our dreams with Godly character.

Most of us have watched tons of reality shows where people share all their everyday life's struggles. We cannot help but to admit that their lives would be better if their day started with prayer and if they recognized that every breath they breathe is by the hands of God. *"The heart of the King is in His hands and He can turn it the way He chooses to do so." (Proverbs 21:1)*

When we recognize this, we will submit to His complete control and then we will see every dark area become illuminated by God's light. Jeremiah 29:12: *"And you shall call upon me, and you shall go and pray to me and I will hear you, you will seek me and find me because you sought me with all your heart."* Please meditate on the above scripture in your devotion and write what God says to you in your journal.

Back to the Future

We know that *Back to the Future* was one of a series of movies directed by Robert Zemeckis. The gist of the story line is Michael Fox tries to change the outcome of situations in the past, present, and future to make sure that his high school age parents unite in order to save his own existence. But we know it is not possible for a human being to stop *time* or to fix the outcome of situations for the greater good of the people. There are times in our life when we just want to play the same character moving through the past, present, and the future to change the outcome for the greater good! But the word of God says again, ***"Forgetting those things that are behind me reaching towards those things in front of me "I press toward the mark of the high calling which is in Christ Jesus"*** *(Philippians 3:13)* The Apostle Paul lets us know that ***"The things that we look in the natural are temporal but when we look to the things that we cannot see they are eternal"*** *(2 Corinthians 4:18)* God is in control over every aspect of our lives the past, present, and future. He is truly alpha and omega (Revelations 1:8). You do not have rewrite your story or change it to fit into society. Just allow God to do His work. He truly holds our entire destiny in His hands and He plays the character of Michael Fox, not us, in the movie *Back to the Future*.

So, if you are reading this book and you are worrying about how God is going to put the broken pieces of your life back together just know that God plays the best part in the movie. He has the final say so and ***If God be for you He is more than the world against you*** (Romans 8:31). Put your best effort forward and just imagine God reaching out His hand to you and you putting your hands in His. Trust that He has total control over your past, present, and your future.

I challenge you today to make a confession that I will no longer wrestle with regrets from the past, the present, or worry about my future. You may be in an incarceration unit and think because you have been sentenced to 20 years that your life is over, but I want to encourage you that your life is not over until God says "It is Over!" When you accept Jesus in your life He will wash away all your sins and put them in the sea of forgetfulness never to remember them any longer! God still has a plan for your life and it is a plan to prosper you for His purpose! (Jeremiah 29:11) You may have an addiction that you have wrestled with all your life but God still has a plan for your life. Your future is not over. When you accept God your life just begins anew! Even when we backslide God forgives us and He does not even remember your sins when you repent. I want you to know that your future is brighter with God because in Him is life and life more abundantly! Our future is truly in the hands of God and not man and He is the ultimate Judge. When man says no, God will say "Yes, I still choose you!"

As I close this chapter, I want you to know that God has chosen your future over your past and your present history. So, let's snap out of our historical lounge pit and move into our future which features the true character of Jesus Christ and His Heavenly host escorting you into a new dimension with His plan for your life! Just say out loud, "I am bringing God into my future!"

This Is It

"This Is It" was the last musical performance done by Michael Jackson, a musical icon and legend of "Pop Music!" After watching the movie, *The Jackson Five* several times I can really identify with Michael when he tells his mother he hears music in his head all the time and that's why he can stay in the studio all day long producing the sound God has given him. In comparison to watching his last video I started to see how the pieces of his story fit together in Michael's musical journey. So *"This is It"* represents his story and encompasses all the beats, all the swings, the moves, and the sounds that God gave Michael Jackson to give to the world. Michael Jackson not only touched the secular world but his life also impacted the Christian world. I remember listening to him and watching him on television as a young girl and being fascinated with how he could move on stage. I have to take a moment and thank God for the gift He placed before all of us and how Michael Jackson, was a true inspiration to every young person. Now please allow me to share with you more about me and my story while in pursuit of God! *This is It, This is My Story……*

This is My Story

I was born and raised in a small city in Rockingham County called Eden, North Carolina on November 21, 1980 to Elder Glenn and Nancy Lewis. Our house was in a suburb community known as

"Piney Fork!" At the age of ten years old, I knew that there was something special God had called me to do. Not just because I was raised in church, or because we were known as the "good girls" but because I was developing a relationship with God during that time.

Primarily I was reared by my parents along with my grandmother. When I was four years old my grandmother would teach me bible scriptures for hours until I was in middle school. We had to memorize almost the whole Bible (lol) and there were times I would say *"Lord can you please deliver me from my grandmother today?"* (lol) But I truly thank God for her teaching and for my parent's fundamental morals that helped me choose the right road. I put God first in everything I did and still do. My decision will always be to pursue God beyond measure!

My parents would always tell me and my brother to give our musical gifts to God and to cultivate the gift God had placed on the inside of us. They trained our ear by letting us hear records like Andrew Crouch, the Hawkins Singers, Vanessa Bell Armstrong, The Winans, The Clark Sisters, Deleon, and many more artists. I truly thank God for my parents and what they imparted in all of us. When I was a child they would constantly play these records. We had only a small amount of time allotted to watch T.V. or play any games but the majority of our time was spent listening to music. Every day our parents worked with us and we would sing the songs back to them. My brother Brent and I are about six years apart and when

He turned 5 or 6 he was singing like He was about double his age. But for me something else was transforming. I was developing an ear to produce music, write music, play instruments, and hear melodies in my head. At ten year's old, I started playing the songs that I heard in my head on all kinds of instruments and I know that it was all God.

Now at the age of 32 years of old, I finally have the opportunity to release my own music projects to the world by the hand of God. I know that it is God's season and time to release the music and sound He has given me to give to the world. I have to admit to you that in my pursuit with God on this narrow road God had me wait for a long time before He would even allow me to send any of my music that I arranged, produced, or wrote to anyone. I have said "No" to several offers in obedience to the will of God and by listening to His voice and I am so glad I chose to obey God and to commit my life to Him. Do not misunderstand me we have all made some mistakes in our lives being hard-headed and choosing to go our own way but thanks be to our God who always causes us to triumph! I went from being hospitalized in psychiatric unit to now a Worship CIA Artist (Center-Stage). To God be the glory! THIS IS IT < THIS IS MY STORY! I My life has been a journey full of joy and serenity to accept those things that I cannot ever change. This is my story. As I close this chapter, I would like you to meditate on the song Blessed Assurance. I encourage you to buy Souls A Fire album so that you can hear the new arrangement I made of Blessed Assurance. You can purchase it online from Oral Roberts University or contact ORU's bookstore.

Eeew, Eeew,
Oooh, Oooh, Oooh, Oooh,
Oooh, Oooh, Oooh, Oooh.
Blessed Assurance
Jesus is Mine,
Oh what a for taste of glory divine,
Heir of salvation,
Purchased by God,
Born of His Spirit,
Washed in His blood,
Oooh, oooh, oooh.
(Back to beginning)
Sop- This is my story
Altos- This is my story
Tenors-This is my story
Yeah My story, my story
This is my story,
Oooh, oooh, oooh,
Ooh, oooh, oooh.
This is my story (Vamp)
Oooh, oooh, oooh, oooh, Oooh

To Be Continued…

Have you ever thought about what would have happened if I had done this? What would have happened if I were here or married this person or not married that person? Is life really a box of chocolates? Do you look at your life through the scope of someone else's life wishing to be in their shoes because you have not taken the risks to step into what God has called you to do? Or maybe there is a voice from your past that is killing your drive to step into your own purpose. There was a message the Lord gave me entitled *"Do not get stuck in traffic"* while other cars are moving in different lanes some of us have missed the sign that says "Go" because we are too busy looking for a hand-out or hand-up! But God designed the abundant life for all His children to possess we just have to stay obedient to His guidance. *He said,* **"I will make your way prosperous"** (Joshua 1:8). Make the right choice to serve God and He will lead you into green pastures.

Psalm 23:1-4; *The Lord is my shepherd and I shall not want. He makes me to lie down in green pastures; He leads me beside the still waters and He restores my soul; he leads me in the paths of righteousness for his name sake. Yea though I walk through the valley of the shadow of death, I will fear no evil, for thou art with me; the rod and staff the comfort me.*

No matter what circumstance we find ourselves facing we should never allow the enemy to cause us not to want to live anymore. In the same way, we see cars in motion on a highway our life is constantly in motion every day. The wind we feel and hear blowing, the birds we hear chirping, the ambulance sirens we hear outside our window are constantly moving because life is still moving. Our life does not stop because of hardships or mistakes that we have made in the past. We still have to continue the journey of faith! It is again the love of God that causes us to get up and fight again.

I just want to recap that as women and men of God when we truly pursue God we will bless the Lord at all times and His praises will continually be in our mouth. In our lives, we may face those dark moments like Job when his entire body was full of boils but He kept saying over and over again "I know my redeemer ***lives, and though He slay me yet will I trust Him, regardless I choose to wait until the appointed time for my change to come!" (Job 19:25; Job 13:15; Job 14:14)***. We are the only ones that can choose to continue to live during life's challenges and obscurities. There is a classic song that was sung by the Clark sisters called **"You are the sunshine in my life"** this song emphasizes the love of God and God being the true center for why we live here on earth. When Christ becomes the sunshine in your life through sickness or health you will still stay anchored in His Word.

I challenge you in this chapter to continue living with the sunshine in your life and to truly trust Him like you have never trusted Him before. God loves you and He has an ultimate plan for your life even in the midst of what you may be facing while reading this book. Jeremiah 29:11 says, ***"For I know the thoughts that I think toward you says Jehovah thoughts of peace and not of evil to give you hope in your latter end."*** *Yes, He has the best plan for you so please choose to continue to live and pursue Him.*

Break the Cycle

While growing up in the church we were told the importance of watching certain patterns in your life to help prevent from making the same mistakes. Someone may be asking the question if the blood of Jesus covers a multitude of sins how could any curse possibly still exist? Although the blood of Jesus exists we have to know what to renounce or what to bind and loose in the Kingdom of God. There are certain territorial demonic spirits that have to be addressed at the root and be renounced by the power of God! Before you get the whole house delivered you have to first bind the strong man and the strong man is not just an image in this parable (Mark 3:27). The *Strong Man* is actually the weaknesses that the enemy has started to attack in a person, family, church, city, or a nation.

One of the major hindrances for people to bind is the strong man. They are afraid to admit strongholds that they have in their family and this prevents them from being capable of breaking the cycle. We have to be completely honest with ourselves in order to truly be delivered from repeating the same cycles in our life. I remember in my twenties God began to deal with me concerning this very issue and the importance of making some better choices to break strongholds from cycling in my own life. As Christian believers, we already have been given the authority we need through the word of God to break every stronghold that has been plaguing our lives, our family, our city, and our nation.

In Mark 5:1-20, there is a parable that Jesus shares about a man who was demon possessed that lived at the cemetery who was full of rage and no one could control him. He was full of so much rage and violence that he would be cutting himself with stones. All day and night he would be at the cemetery screaming out in the woods. When you do extensive research on this parable we find that this man was psychotic, he actually was dealing with a schizophrenia disorder according to Dr. Steven Waterhouse (And demonic oppression). But when he saw Jesus the man snapped out of his oppression and began to cry out and worship Him. And Jesus told him *"What do you need?"* And the demons replied (instead of the man) *"Please do not torment us."* Jesus said, *"Come out of him you unclean spirit, what is your name?"* The demons replied again, **"Legion"** for we are many (Legion is a military term 3000 or more soldiers). As Jesus began to exercise His authority every unclean spirit came out of the man and went into the swine. The demon-possessed man was totally delivered from all his oppression and his mind was fully restored. The text begins to explain after his miraculous encounter with Jesus he began to evangelize the same city by sharing his story with others.

As Christian believer's just as we know the *Bill of Rights* of this country and we understand how to fight for our rights. If our rights have been violated in the Kingdom of God we have to know our God given rights so that we can exercise our authority against the enemy. For example, if someone fires you unjustly from your job and it's a discrimination issue you would file a civil lawsuit against this matter to fight for your justice. In the same manner, on a consistent basis we have to walk in our authority as citizens of the Kingdom of God. Luke 10:19 says, ***"Behold I have given you all power and authority in heaven and on earth to tread upon serpents and scorpions and all of the power of the enemy and nothing shall be able to harm you."***

We have been redeemed from the law of the curse through the blood of Jesus but we have to activate our power through the word of God to close all doors to the enemy (Galatians 3:13). We have to break the cycles that we see after recognizing them whether it be the spirit of abuse, the spirit of alcohol addiction, adultery, murder, spirit of violence, spirit of fear, spirit of intimidation, spirit of control, spirit of lying, spirit of lust, spirit of covetness, or spirit of stealing. These spirits have to be bound through the word of God and the doorways have to be closed through the blood of Jesus. We have to renounce the spirits and their influence on our families.

I challenge you as I close this chapter to commit to be totally honest and ask the Holy Spirit to reveal to you what cycles have been plaguing you, your family, your city, your nation and begin to renounce their demonic activity and close these doorways through the blood of Jesus. We agree in the name of Jesus Christ that the cycle is now broken in every area of our life.

The Price is Right!

We know *"The Price is Right"* is a well-known television show that used to feature one of the best hosts known as Robert (Bob) Barker. Each contestant from the audience would have the opportunity to bid for all kinds of items for money and other materials. People from all walks of life for several years have watched this television show because it gave people a sense of hope and joy to see those who may not have been on the other side of life to have a chance to live what we call *The Good life*. Some people are still bidding in life hoping to get the right price not knowing that Jesus has truly paid the ultimate price. You do not have to gamble any more, you do not have to sell drugs any more to get ahead in life, you do not have to sleep around for money anymore. You do not have to bid through the world's system to have *"The Good life."* You do not have to sell your soul to Satan, you do not have to back-stab your way to the top because the ladder starts and ends with Christ who is the head of the Church. He is the top-bidder and since He already knew the price He purchased it a long time ago. He may not come through on your time, but He will be on *kairos* time which is the time of Heaven.

The Bids of Life
We have all anticipated going to auctions waiting on our turn to get the chance to bid on the item we want. Many people leave the auction proud to get what they

wanted at the amount they could afford instead of having to use another means which may have been more-costly. But we have to understand that there are some things that should not be on display for us to bid for in life. Some people bid on other people's husbands, boyfriends, other people's homes and other possessions not realizing that they are only damaging themselves. Some people even bid for others to fail not understanding the biblical principle that ***"Whatever you sow you will reap"*** (Galatians: 6-8). It is God who is in control and not man. In our pursuit of God we cannot manipulate God on a bid that is not a biblical principle. Neither can we pay our way to heaven's door. The rich man asked Jesus ***"How do I inherit the kingdom of God? What do I have to do?*** Jesus replied, ***"Give everything that you have to the poor and then follow me"*** (Matthew 19:21). This does not mean that God wanted him to become poor but it gives us the concept to put Him first in our life and what His heart calls us to do for the Kingdom of God. We are blessed to be a blessing to others. According to Deuteronomy 28:1, ***"God will command the blessing to be upon all those who hearken diligently to the voice of the Lord, to observe and to do all his commandments which he will give and He will set us high above the nations of the earth."***

As I close this chapter, I want you to understand that when God made the world His only desire was to see man bid only on Him. He said, come to me those who are broken-hearted, empty, poor, widowed, orphaned, lonely, rejected, homeless, jobless, un-loved, un-appreciated, whatever it is know that God has your price tag and now, "The Price is Right."

He's Coming Back

On several occasions, many of us have become aware of the signs of the end time as we have turned on the daily news and hear all about the famines, the earthquakes, and wars that are happening in diverse places. But before the end is here, Matthew 24:14 tells us that the Gospel will be preached in the entire world then the world will end. But we do not know the day or the hour when Christ will return for His pride so we have to stay ready (Mark 13:32). Ephesians 5:27 also tells us that He is coming for a pure vessel that the church should be without spot or wrinkle. When we pursue God, it is very important that we understand that it is for a great reward because Christ is coming back to give us a crown of glory! (Matthew 24:49) *This is good news*! When we lay down our life for God we will gain it back in the end not just in wealth and material possessions but when we hear Him say ***"Well done my good and faithful servant, you have been faithful over a few things, you will now become ruler over many things in My Kingdom"*** (Matthew 25:23).

I remember while living on the campus of ORU one of my preferred scriptures that I placed on my wall was Galatians 2:20 ***"I have been crucified with Christ, and it is no longer I that live, but Christ lives in me, and the life which I now live in the flesh I live in faith which is in the Son of God, who loved me, and gave himself up for me."*** This was the biblical scripture that I studied that kept me rooted and grounded in my faith journey and led me to the place of my promise. When I would get weak in my faith I would just meditate on that scripture and it would always put me back on track especially when I lost my father three months before graduating college. I remember hearing the spirit tell me *"You love your father, but I love him more."* This changed my life forever because I no longer saw life the same anymore. We all have to admit that sometimes it gets hard in our faith journey but we can be reassured that Christ is coming back to wipe away all our tears. We will no longer feel pain or hurt. It gives me confidence to know that my dad who suffered for so long from diabetes and congestive heart failure does not have to get another needle stuck in his arm again. It was so hard for me to see him in the hospital constantly in pain. I think one of my greatest challenges before he died was when he had to get his foot amputated. But I still give praise to the Lord because now he has a new foot and it will not ever have to be removed. I just want to encourage you if you are reading this book and you have a loved one who needs healing, or you have a disease that has been ailing you or maybe you are at that point where you are contemplating your faith in God because you have been so hurt by someone or something be encouraged to know that your *"Heavenly Father"* is coming back to rescue you! There is a place that has been prepared just for you that has your name written on it in Heaven (St. John 14:1-3).

Live for Eternity
Every day we should be living for eternity and not just for ourselves. We have to make our life count so God's glory will be revealed on earth. When we die we should not be just known by our parents but by the works we have done through Christ and exuberating His character. Matthew 5:16 says ***"Let your light so shine that men may see your good works and glorify your Father which is in Heaven."*** Through the guidance of the Holy Spirit He will lead you to where to serve and how to live a life that totally pleases Him. There was a message that I once heard at ORU chapel that stirred my heart so much that I will never forget it. The question our chaplain asked us was *"When you die what will people say about you at your funeral?" (Hosea Maralez)* I thought this was a very deep philosophical question to ask college students but on the inside my heart was stirring up through the Holy Spirit. It became a reality that we are not here on earth to just exist but that we have purpose to fulfill before Christ returns! God is speaking to us, yes, He is speaking loud to the CHURCH known as the *Ecclesia* the governing body of Christ. Will you answer His call before He returns? You are His hands, you are His feet, you are His mouthpiece, and you are His masterpiece. The clock is still moving right now and God needs more people to work in His vineyard to win more *souls* for His kingdom.

As I began to evaluate my personal life at that time listening to that message it confirmed to me how serious this Christian walk is and how our lives can really have a significant impact on others. Will you make your life count for Christ's return? I hope you will say yes because our Heavenly Father is coming back and He will be the supreme judge, not man, who will judge our works while we are here on earth. We see a foreshadowing of this in the book of Revelations when John reveals the seven seals from God to speak to each church in regards to their work and character. So this is an appeal to the body of Christ in 2013 to allow the Holy Spirit to prepare you for Christ's coming and move you in your divine position. Do not allow your yesterday to impact your today or tomorrow! Each week we should be putting a demand on how many souls to bring to God through the Holy Spirit. Earlier today, I was just sharing with my mother how Jehovah witnesses have more zeal to evangelize people than Christians and this should not be! Christian believers should be the majority that will knock on our neighbor's doors with pamphlets in our hands sharing the true Gospel of Jesus Christ.

As I close this chapter, I challenge you today as you are reading this book to think of 2 people each week that you can share the love of God with and sow the seed of the Gospel and win a soul for Christ.

Your Road to Recovery

As I began this chapter, I find it very intriguing that when I initially typed this subtitle I originally was going to call it *"Your Road to Victory"* but then I heard the Lord say *"No"* name it *"Your Road to Recovery"* because there is a distinct difference between the terms victory and recovery. When we use the word *victory* it refers to "the overcoming of an enemy or antagonist, an achievement of mastery or success in a struggle or endeavor against odds or difficulties" (Merriam Webster Dictionary, 1). But the word *recover* goes a step further and has several implications which are the following 1. "The act or process to be free from sickness or a setback; recuperation 2. Restoration to a former or better condition 3. The regaining of something lost 4. The extraction of useful substances from waste. 5. Law: Obtaining of a right by the judgment of a court b. the final judgment or verdict in a case (Free Online Dictionary, 1). "Yes we can look at these implications and see that the word *recovery* can mean various things according to our situation. You may be wondering how will I ever get out of this dilemma? It may be that you have cancer or you may have been laid off from your job or dealing with a broken relationship but God can take the extraction of useful substances from His kingdom *to* bring recovery to your life. The word of God tells us that He will give us back ***"Everything that the locusts has stolen and the cankerworm has eaten up and you shall have***

plenty and be satisfied" (Joel 2:25). God has the final say in your case and He will execute the verdict on your account so that you can be released! You may be saying, "You do not know how long I have been dealing with this situation and in the natural it seems like it is not getting any better!" His Word says ***"Weeping may endure for a night but joy comes in the morning"*** (Psalm 30:5).

What you may have thought was a set-back or a trauma in your life is a set-up! God will sometimes allow situations to come into our life only to reveal His glory. In the book of St. John 11 chapter, a man by the name of Lazarus was so sick that He died but Jesus kept saying over and over ***"This sickness is not for death but to reveal God's glory"*** (St. John 11:4). Lazarus sisters were disarrayed to find out that their only brother had died but Jesus told them ***"I am the resurrection and the life and those who believe in me will have everlasting life"*** (John 11:25) The sister responded by telling Jesus ***"Yes I do believe that you are the resurrection and the life!"*** (St. John 11:27) This same question that Christ asked them He is still asking us today. Do you still believe that I am the resurrection and the life? Do you still believe that I can restore your situation so that you will have *total recovery*? It does not matter how long we have been in the situation or what kind of case it is or how much that relationship meant to us! When God steps on the scene in one second everything can CHANGE!

When Christ went to find where Lazarus was laid at the tomb he only said three words ***"LAZARUS COME FORTH!"*** The man who was underground buried for four days instantly came up from out of the grave with his garments around him. God is going to bring total recovery from every Lazarus situation that has ever attacked our life. Then He is going to release us to go share our story for His glory! We cannot give up or give in to Satan's lies that tell us that we will be in this pit for the remainder of our life. You have to still believe God and He is waiting on you to say "God I trust you to be my resurrection and my life giver." Then the road to recovery will begin to unveil in your life and you will see how this small step that you took will begin to later turn into a milestone. It may be tough when you begin to deal with your flesh and its craving to want to move in the opposite direction that God is telling you but you need to stay on the road. Do not turn around. Do not take a detour or get in another car with another driver. Let Him still be the overseer of your life! The road may get rocky and you may even see some deer on the side of the road that may try to cross traffic. Trust God. Trust God in your pain, trust God in your financial dilemmas, trust God in your health, in your marriage, in your relationships, and in your family. Whatever it is know that you are on your road to recover all! Lazarus was not just completely healed but He was totally recovered! The last words Jesus said to the guards on behalf of Lazarus was to *"Loose Him and Let Him Go!"* (St. John 11:43-44).

Please recognize that on your road to recovery that you have been truly loosed from even the smell and the residue of what you have been through. Just like the grave clothes on Lazarus had to be taken away from him and the ropes that once tied his feet and his arms were released. You have been released from the hands of the enemy's snares. You are free and no longer bound to be a slave to your situation. Your recovery has come by your faith in the plan of God and the fact that He is Sovereign.

I challenge you as read this chapter to remain on the road to recovery with God as the driver of your life!

The Final Rebound

Most of us enjoy watching the game of basketball being played by our favorite team players especially when they are in the final quarter and the winning team gets the rebound shot! You may not even recognize it but you are in *the final quarter of "the game of life"* and God will make the final rebound shot for you! He is making the rebound shots for each one of our disappointments and just as we see in the natural the ball bouncing from an *"unsuccessful shot"* God is retrieving the ball to make a successful play! God is resounding the alarm very loud in our life to enter the game again to win!

Get in the Game
When we were children playing with our next door neighbors and siblings everyone would be having a good time until one of us would lose and say **"*I don't want to play this game anymore, I am going in the house!*"** Some of us would get so angry about losing the game with our playmates that we would refuse to even play anymore. When we were children playing with our next door neighbors and siblings everyone would be having a good time until one of us would lose and say **"*I don't want to play this game anymore, I am going in the house!*"** Some of us would get so angry about losing the game with our playmates that we would refuse to even play anymore. How many times have you treated God the same way? Refusing to get in the game and staying in our own safe haven.

You hear the children outside your door playing, being loud having fun, dribbling the ball on the court, screaming at one another, the basketball rim being hit, and the ball falling through the nets. You come outside and the kids are shouting your name "AMY" please come play the game with us, play on our team, we need more players on our team!

What is preventing you from getting in the game of life? Are you tired of playing due to first, second, or third quarter? It is now the fourth quarter and it's time for you to allow God to revive your soul so that you can be in His game again. There are people that are waiting for you that He has ordained for you to help on the court. They cannot be an official team without you and it is time for you to come off the bench. In the *"Game of Life"* there is a constant spiritual warfare between the soul and the spirit trying to keeping us from winning the shots. But when we pursue God we have to walk in the spirit and then we will not fulfill the lust of our flesh. Our mind has to be renewed on a consistent basis through the word of God (Romans 12:1-2). You may be saying this is an impossible task to do while dealing with the pressures of life but you are more than a conqueror through Jesus Christ who loves you! (Romans 8:37) You have to make a commitment to be on the winning side of the game by throwing the ball totally to God and then just get ready for the *slam dunk!* Can you feel the blood running warm *again* in your veins?

The depression that once controlled you, the addiction that once controlled you, the debt that controlled you, that woman or man that held you captive no longer exist because you have put on your game gear with God who has resuscitated you!

In the Book of Kings 2:4 there was a Shunammite woman who would take care of the prophet Elisha every time he came to minister in the area. She would allow him to stay at her home. This woman understood the position and authority of God's prophets. Matthew 10:20 says, *"**He that receives a prophet in the name of a prophet shall receive a prophet's reward, and he that receives a righteous man in the name of a righteous man shall receive a righteous man's reward.**"* The Bible also says that she even made an extra room in her house for Elisha to stay so that he would feel at home when he returned from ministering to so many people in the city.

Later on the prophet told her that God was going to give her a son by a certain time and that He would open up her womb. The woman told him, **"*Do not lie to me,*"** and He told her **"*I am not, you will have a son.*"** The word of God prevailed and the woman and her husband had a son. But the parable goes on to say that one day the boy was out with his dad in the field and he started to touch his head and say **"*Father, Father My Head!*"** It does not state what kind of illness that the young boy had but we know it was detrimental to his health because he died.

The child's parents were devastated. When Elisha the prophet came to the city again the child's mother was trying to get in contact with Gehazi his servant. Gehazi came back to their home with the prophet's staff and put it along the child's face but the child still did not move.

Then the Bible says that Gehazi called for Elisha and when he got there he went up to a room for prayer. *"And then he went up and lay upon the child put his mouth upon his mouth, and his eyes upon his eyes, and his hands upon his hands, and he stretched himself upon him, and the child sneezed seven times, and the child opened his eyes (1 Kings 4: 34-35).* God has the power to resuscitate you, just as this child was brought back to life for every situation that has brought you down to your lowest point. God will take the shot to bring you back up again. He will breath His spirit into your nostrils, He will stretch Himself out on your entire circumstance! Your life is not destined for defeat, but it is destined for greatness! So, set your eyes far above for a brighter future because God is going to exceed your imagination and expectations of what He unveils in your life.

The Golden Eagle

As I write to you again, it is now approximately 6:57 pm on January 21, 2013 Martin Luther King Jr.'s birthday and the inauguration of President Barack Obama! What an awesome day to celebrate the dream, the legacy, and witness the mantel being passed down to the next generation. When we reflect on these moments it should give us a sense of hope that every day we have the chance to make a difference in this world. In our pursuit of God and His call on our lives it is not always easy but we can see through the lives of Jesus, Martin Luther King Jr, President Barack Obama, and several others that the mission can be accomplished! There are many character traits that these men had which can be compared to a *golden eagle*. Most *golden eagles* "spend their *time gliding* and when they dive groundward it is very interesting to know that they can reach speeds of 240-320, and the nests that they build are for more than one *generation*."
(www.nature.ca/notebooks/english/gldeagle.htm, 1). If you are reading this book know that you have the potential to become a "golden eagle" and that there are doors waiting for you to rise to the occasion. So in this final chapter we will deal with those underlying roots that try to hinder you from becoming the *golden eagle*.

The Castaway Mentality

Have you ever found yourself making up excuses for not fulfilling obligations and responsibilities? You basically chose to avoid or ignore whatever the matter was instead of confronting the real issue. There are also people in this world who refuse to seize the opportunities that life brings them because they are carrying a spirit of rejection. Someone may have told you in the past that you are not smart enough, that you did not have the proper education, or that you do not fit the part so you may be living your life as a *cast away*. People who live with a *Castaway Mentality* find it hard to break away from the eagle's nest and this does not mean just leaving from your parent's house. The *Castaway Mentality* goes much farther than just your physical location but it is about your spiritual location and your passion for pursing God and His call on your life! A *Castaway Mentality* limits you from rising like the eagle because you refuse to let go of what someone said that tries to cripple you each time an opportunity comes. If that is you and you are reading this book please get out a pen and paper and begin to write down all the people or the situations that made you feel rejected, unwanted, and devalued. Then immediately ask God to help you forgive them and He will heal all of your wounds that have caused a spirit of rejection to come upon you and release His spirit of might upon you! I decree to you that you are no longer "*A Castaway*" but you are king or queen in the kingdom of God and you are a *golden eagle*!

The Runaway Mentality

As you are read this subtitle *The Runaway Mentality* you maybe recalling a time in your life that reflects a certain action or situation. Please be encouraged you are not alone because I am also recalling many occasions when I was a *Runaway!* You may be also raising a child that is dealing with *The Runaway Mentality*. What do you do? How do handle this one? Ok so what is the *Runaway Mentality,* when we refuse to listen or obey the voice of God, or the voice of God given by authority because we do not want to totally surrender to His call on our lives.

Yes, I have to really admit that before I surrendered to God's call I was rebellious in high school but still there was a small voice speaking to me even when I was in the *stage of rebellion*. There are people who are young and old that find themselves for various reasons not fully obeying God even though they know the consequence is destruction. If we continually refuse to obey God regardless of what age we are we will find ourselves still pecking at the nest instead of developing into the *golden eagle*.

In the Book of Jonah, we see that he also struggled with the spirit of rebellion. He was a "Runaway" because he refused to go back to Nineveh to preach the gospel to the people and he did not like the people because they were disobedient. However, this man found himself being trapped by God in the belly of a fish and totally having to surrender to the call

of God. How much more will it take for you? Will it cost you your life to finally surrender to the call? How many more times will your parents have to keep reminding you about making better choices? Do not let it be another time that you allow someone else over God or your parents to lead you. Make the better choice and stop being a runaway because God's design is for you to become His golden eagle. Some of you may be saying while reading this book I am tired of running in my life and all the turns I have been through. I am tired of making the same mistakes choosing to go my own way instead of His way and I want out! If that's you and you truly want out then you can be free.

I decree to you today as you are reading this book that the spirit of rebellion will no longer rule your life but the fear of the Lord will permeate your heart. You will be sensitive to the Spirit and the things of God. If God did it for me, He can do it for you.

The Eagle's Mentality

Do you have the mind of an *eagle*? A person who is *strong-willed* just like an eagle can soar far (high) above the obstacles or circumstances they face in life. They know how to adjust and keep the right altitude and demeanour to keep soaring. An eagle's wings are able to spread and glide to their designated destinations. Just like an eagle how do we spread our wings and take flight? Instead of drawing back when you are faced with unwanted troubles draw near to God and you will begin to fly again. *Eagles* do not spend any of their time on the ground instead they spend their time flying in the sky!

Eagles think "BIG" they do not have the mediocre, average level of thinking because they can see beyond the normal capacity. Eagles only hang out with eagles they do not hang out with ground-hoppers. When you are an eagle God gives you the ability to glide through every *time bomb* set by the enemy He will lead you by His speed and Satan will not be able to even touch you. The pressure that an eagle feels when he is soaring does not cause the eagle to get off course. Instead eagles just glide right through spreading their wings wider as they move to a higher altitude. In the same manner, a pilot moves a plane higher to avoid too much turbulence I encourage you to take flight on some of the *unwanted pressures* that you find yourself facing in life and use them to catapult you to your *next dimension* in God. Then you will find yourself soaring like a *golden eagle*!

The heroes of faith and our modern-day heroes as Martin Luther King Jr. and President Barack Obama are all golden eagles because they possess the same attributes to expand their vision in spite of the opposition that have come against their God ordained assignment. These heroes were BIG thinkers, visionaries, and most of all they had integrity. It is these attributes that caused them and several others to effectively build their "nests" for the next generations. When we pursue God with our whole heart it should cause us to look at our own needs as well as the *needs of others*.

As we truly pursue God by seeking His face, His hand, and His heart we will be able to leave something behind for the next generation. Something that is tangible from God so they can see the hand of God upon the work of our hands. I am determined with everything on the inside of me that my children, grandchildren, and great-grandchildren will be able to carry on their Heavenly assignments by God. They will be able to witness what happened in their mother and grandmother's life. In order for us to build our eagle's nests effectively it has to start with our relationship with the Lord. The next generation needs you and me to become lights and examples of obedience to the will of God. The purpose of God should be our driving motivation (or motivational force) that causes us to soar like *golden eagles* far above until we accomplish all our Heavenly assignments.

I challenge you as you are reading this book, to build your nests with agape love, with God's Word, and the fruit of the Spirit. It takes courage and boldness to carry the torch of God but in the end, we will be able to see Him face to face, just to hear Him say, ***"Well done my good and faithful servant"*** (Matthew 25:21) You kept going, you kept believing, you kept pursuing me more than what the world could offer you because *You loved Me. My child, guess what? You found Me.*

Living a Life Full of Passion for God

As you have read this book, I pray that it has compelled you to live a life

Full of Passion for God and that you will experience God with

A new zeal and make a lifetime commitment to do His will.

When we pursue God it should not be for what we can obtain but to

Become more like Him and to reveal His Shekinah glory in the earth! This

time when you go to an award's ceremony and you hear all the names being

called out do not forget the real honoree which is "Jesus Christ, the Son of the Living God!"

To God be the glory for all the things that He has done! Selah

Bibliography

The Bible: Amplified & KJV & NIV Versions

"Consistent." **www.google.com**

Culbertson, Howard. 10/40 Window: "Do you need to be stirred to action? How many in the world have never heard the gospel?" Southern Nazarene

University. *Page 1/April 1996*

http.home.snu.edu

"Domestic Violence." What is Fast Facts on Domestic Violence.www.clarkprosecutor.org.

Retrieved September 3, 2015.

Family." Page 1 of Mother Theresa/Christian Fathers "Go home and love your family."

www.christianfathers.com Retrieved April 2, 2013.

Frost, Robert. "The Road Less Traveled." A New Psychology of Love, Traditional Values and Spiritual Growth. By M. Scott Peck, MD. Touchstone book published Simon & Schuster, 1978. NY, NY.

Hungerford, Margaret. Beauty if in the Eye of the Beholder." Page 142 "Molly Bawn."1878.

Lipka, Michael. "What surveys say about worship attendance-and why some stay home." Retrieved September 2013 from htpp://www.pewresearch.org.

"Jesus is mentioned."
www.whatChristianswanttoknow.com. Page 35. Retrieved 9 September 2014. Retrieved July 2, 2014.

"Recovery."
www.freeonlinedictionary.com/recovery. Retrieved February 11, 2016.

"Reputation" and "Victory" Word Central: Merriam Webster's Student's Electronic Dictionary. 2001.http: **www.ww.m.com/dictionary.htm**

3 June 2014.

"Submission." Greek Lexicon.

"Submission." Strong's Concordance.

Waterhouse, Dr. Steven. "Strength for His people."

www.schizophrenia.com/media/strength/htm.Retrived February 11, 2016.

Nystrom, Marty. "As the Deer."

www.hymnary.org/person/nystrom_m.

Retrieved March 3 2014.

Vandross, Luther & Richard Marx. "Dance with my father." Released 2003/ www.metrolyrics.com/dance. Retrieved July 9, 2014.

Youngblood, Ronald. Bruce, F.F. Harrison, RK, & Thomas Nelson Publishers (1995). Thomas Nelson Bible Dictionary. Three Types of Love, Page 775. Nashville, TN.

Made in the USA
San Bernardino, CA
21 June 2017